Mockito Essentials

A practical guide to get you up and running with unit testing using Mockito

Sujoy Acharya

PUBLISHING

BIRMINGHAM - MUMBAI

Mockito Essentials

Copyright © 2014 Packt Publishing

First published: October 2014

Production reference: 1171014

Published by Packt Publishing Ltd.
Livery Place
35 Livery Street
Birmingham B3 2PB, UK.

ISBN 978-1-78398-360-5

www.packtpub.com

Cover image by Asher Wishkerman (wishkerman@hotmail.com)

Credits

Author
Sujoy Acharya

Reviewers
Christian Baranowski
Tim Perry
Gualtiero Testa

Commissioning Editor
Amarabha Banerjee

Acquisition Editor
James Jones

Content Development Editor
Pooja Nair

Technical Editor
Humera Shaikh

Copy Editors
Dipti Kapadia
Shambhavi Pai

Project Coordinator
Leena Purkait

Proofreaders
Simran Bhogal
Cathy Cumberlidge

Indexers
Mariammal Chettiyar
Tejal Soni

Graphics
Sheetal Aute
Abhinash Sahu

Production Coordinator
Shantanu N. Zagade

Cover Work
Alwin Roy

About the Author

Sujoy Acharya works as a software architect with Siemens Technology and Services Pvt. Ltd. (STS). He grew up in a joint family and pursued his graduation in the field of Computer Science and Engineering. His hobbies are watching movies and sitcoms, playing outdoor sports, and reading books.

Sujoy likes to research on upcoming technologies. His major contributions are in the field of Java, J2EE, SOA, Ajax, GWT, and Spring Framework.

Sujoy has authored two books, *Test-Driven Development with Mockito* and *Mastering Unit Testing Using Mockito and JUnit*, both by Packt Publishing.

Sujoy designs and develops healthcare software products. He has over 11 years of industrial experience and has architected and implemented large-scale enterprise solutions.

I'd especially like to thank my wife, Sunanda, for pushing me to man up and finish the book, for her patience, and for her endless support for the many hours she spent reviewing my draft and providing valuable inputs.

I would also like to thank my mother and my late father for their support, blessings, and encouragement.

To my 20-month-old kid, Abhigyan: I am sorry, I couldn't be around you as much as we all wanted and had to get you away from the laptop many times. I love you very much.

About the Reviewers

Christian Baranowski is a project manager and software architect with SEITENBAU, a midsized (120 employees) web agency, software development company, and IT service provider. SEITENBAU's core areas of expertise are web development, deployment and customization of content management systems, the development of enterprise and employee portals, as well as customer-specific software development. Christian leads a team of developers, and he describes his role at SEITENBAU as an agile developer and tester. He has blogged and spoken at a wide variety of conferences on web development, OSGi, and testing. When he is not working, you'll find him spending time with his wife, son, and daughter.

Tim Perry is a technical lead and the open source champion at Softwire (a bespoke software development company in North London). By day, he is guiding teams, building a variety of great software at every scale for his clients, and pushing Softwire to engage with and give back to the wider software development community. He works with a huge range of tools daily, from Java, Spring, and JUnit to JavaScript web components and SQL analytics engines.

By night, he's a frequent technical speaker, and a prolific open source contributor to a huge variety of projects, including JUnit, Mockito, Knockout, and Lodash, and some of his own, such as loglevel and grunt-coveralls. Tim is feverishly keen on all things related to automated testing, polyglot persistence, as well as good, old-fashioned, high-quality software development.

I'd like to thank my wonderful girlfriend, Rachel, for her endless patience and support and for genuinely appearing delighted when I signed up for yet another side project.

Gualtiero Testa is a software analyst, architect, and developer involved in Java enterprise-level web applications, mainly in the banking, health, and government agencies' domain.

His main interests are Test-driven Development (TDD), testing tools and methodologies, and everything related to code quality. He can be reached through his blog at `http://www.gualtierotesta.it/`. He lives in Pavia, Italy.

I would like to thank my wife for her constant support, encouragement, and patience.

www.PacktPub.com

Support files, eBooks, discount offers, and more

You might want to visit www.PacktPub.com for support files and downloads related to your book.

Did you know that Packt offers eBook versions of every book published, with PDF and ePub files available? You can upgrade to the eBook version at www.PacktPub.com and as a print book customer, you are entitled to a discount on the eBook copy. Get in touch with us at service@packtpub.com for more details.

At www.PacktPub.com, you can also read a collection of free technical articles, sign up for a range of free newsletters and receive exclusive discounts and offers on Packt books and eBooks.

http://PacktLib.PacktPub.com

Do you need instant solutions to your IT questions? PacktLib is Packt's online digital book library. Here, you can access, read and search across Packt's entire library of books.

Why subscribe?
- Fully searchable across every book published by Packt
- Copy and paste, print and bookmark content
- On demand and accessible via web browser

Free access for Packt account holders

If you have an account with Packt at www.PacktPub.com, you can use this to access PacktLib today and view nine entirely free books. Simply use your login credentials for immediate access.

Table of Contents

Preface

We can acquire knowledge in different ways. On one side is theory, and on the other side is the application of theory. Both are important and both make us better. Theoretical knowledge can provide us with a deep understanding of the concept through the experiences of others, but a practical application can give us a deep understanding through the reality of life and the act of doing.

I was looking for a Mockito framework guide that could teach me the practical application of the framework, but I didn't find any book or article. Then, I decided to start writing a book that can focus on both the theoretical aspect and the practical application, so that readers can get a deep understanding of the concepts through the act of doing.

This book is an advanced-level guide that will help software developers to get complete expertise in unit testing using Mockito as the mocking framework. The focus of the book is to provide readers with comprehensive details on how effectively Mockito can be used for mocking external dependencies in Java application, web application, legacy code, GWT, and SOA.

Armed with the knowledge of advanced JUnit concepts and mocking framework essentials, you will be pleasantly surprised at how quickly and easily you can write high-quality, clean, readable, testable, maintainable, and extensible code.

What this book covers

Chapter 1, *Exploring Test Doubles*, covers the concept of automated unit tests, talks about the characteristics of a good unit test, and explores the test's doubles. It provides examples of dummy objects, fake objects, stubs, mock objects, and spies.

Chapter 2, Socializing with Mockito, focuses on getting the reader quickly started with the Mockito overview, unit test qualities, and the significance of Mockito in unit testing. It also explains and provides examples of stubbing, answering, throwing exceptions, argument matchers, and method call verification. The Mockito architecture is also uncovered.

Chapter 3, Accelerating Mockito, illustrates advanced Mockito framework topics, such as working with void methods, throwing exceptions from void methods, writing callbacks for void methods, returning values using doReturn, void method chaining, calling original methods, Mockito annotations, verifying arguments using an argument captor, verifying an invocation order, spying objects using spy, changing default Mockito settings, resetting mock objects, inline stubbing, and mock details.

Chapter 4, Behavior-driven Development with Mockito, unfolds the BDD concepts, BDD examples, and writing BDD style tests with Mockito.

Chapter 5, Unit Testing the Legacy Code with Mockito, explores legacy code, testing impediments, design for testability, and unit testing the legacy code with Mockito and PowerMock. By the end of this chapter, the reader will be able to write JUnit tests for a legacy code with Mockito and PowerMock, refactor the legacy code to make it unit testable, and design code to bypass the testing impediments.

Chapter 6, Developing SOA with Mockito, deals with web services, explores SOAP and RESTful web services with examples, and helps us to write JUnit tests for the web services with Mockito to mock out the web service framework dependencies.

Chapter 7, Unit Testing GWT Code with Mockito, provides an overview of Ajax/GWT, explains the MVP pattern and loose coupling, and provides examples and strategies to mock GWT widgets using Mockito.

What you need for this book

You will need the following software to be installed before running the examples in this book:

- **Java 7 or higher**: JDK 1.7 or higher can be downloaded from the Oracle site at `http://www.oracle.com/technetwork/java/javase/downloads/index.html`.
- **Eclipse editor**: The latest version of Eclipse is Luna (4.4.1). Luna can be downloaded from `http://www.eclipse.org/downloads/`.
- **Mockito**: Mockito is required for the creation and verification of mock objects and for stubbing. Mockito can be downloaded from `https://code.google.com/p/mockito/downloads/list`.

Who this book is for

This book is for advanced to novice level software testers/developers using Mockito in the JUnit framework, with a reasonable knowledge level and understanding of unit testing elements and applications.

It is ideal for developers who have some experience in Java application development as well as some basic knowledge of JUnit testing, but it covers the basic fundamentals of JUnit testing and the Mockito framework to get you acquainted with these concepts before using them.

Conventions

In this book, you will find a number of styles of text that distinguish between different kinds of information. Here are some examples of these styles, and an explanation of their meaning.

Code words in text, database table names, folder names, filenames, file extensions, pathnames, dummy URLs, user input, and Twitter handles are shown as follows: "Tests should be readable and expressive; for example, a test that verifies unauthorized access can be written as `testUnauthorizedAccess()` or rather `when_an_unauthorized_user_accesses_the_system_then_raises_secuirty_error()`."

A block of code is set as follows:

```
@Test
  public void currencyRoundsOff() throws Exception {
    assertNotNull(CurrencyFormatter.format(100.999));
    assertTrue(CurrencyFormatter.format(100.999).contains("$"));
    assertEquals("$101.00", CurrencyFormatter.format(100.999));
  }
```

When we wish to draw your attention to a particular part of a code block, the relevant lines or items are set in bold:

```
public class LocaleTest {
  private Locale defaultLocale;
  @Before
  public void setUp() {
    defaultLocale = Locale.getDefault();
    Locale.setDefault(Locale.GERMANY);
  }
  @After
  public void restore() {
    Locale.setDefault(defaultLocale);
```

```
    }
    @Test
    public void currencyRoundsOff() throws Exception {
        assertEquals("$101.00", CurrencyFormatter.format(100.999));
    }
}
```

New terms and **important words** are shown in bold. Words that you see on the screen, in menus or dialog boxes for example, appear in the text like this: "Go to the **Libraries** tab in the project's build path."

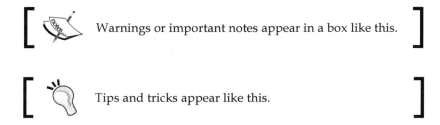

Warnings or important notes appear in a box like this.

Tips and tricks appear like this.

Reader feedback

Feedback from our readers is always welcome. Let us know what you think about this book—what you liked or may have disliked. Reader feedback is important for us to develop titles that you really get the most out of.

To send us general feedback, simply send an e-mail to feedback@packtpub.com, and mention the book title via the subject of your message.

If there is a topic that you have expertise in and you are interested in either writing or contributing to a book, see our author guide on www.packtpub.com/authors.

Customer support

Now that you are the proud owner of a Packt book, we have a number of things to help you to get the most from your purchase.

Downloading the example code

You can download the example code files for all Packt books you have purchased from your account at http://www.packtpub.com. If you purchased this book elsewhere, you can visit http://www.packtpub.com/support and register to have the files e-mailed directly to you.

Downloading the color images of this book

We also provide you a PDF file that has color images of the screenshots/diagrams used in this book. The color images will help you better understand the changes in the output. You can download this file from https://www.packtpub.com/sites/default/files/downloads/3605OS_Graphics.pdf.

Errata

Although we have taken every care to ensure the accuracy of our content, mistakes do happen. If you find a mistake in one of our books — maybe a mistake in the text or the code — we would be grateful if you would report this to us. By doing so, you can save other readers from frustration and help us improve subsequent versions of this book. If you find any errata, please report them by visiting http://www.packtpub.com/submit-errata, selecting your book, clicking on the **errata submission form** link, and entering the details of your errata. Once your errata are verified, your submission will be accepted and the errata will be uploaded on our website, or added to any list of existing errata, under the Errata section of that title. Any existing errata can be viewed by selecting your title from http://www.packtpub.com/support.

Piracy

Piracy of copyright material on the Internet is an ongoing problem across all media. At Packt, we take the protection of our copyright and licenses very seriously. If you come across any illegal copies of our works, in any form, on the Internet, please provide us with the location address or website name immediately so that we can pursue a remedy.

Please contact us at copyright@packtpub.com with a link to the suspected pirated material.

We appreciate your help in protecting our authors, and our ability to bring you valuable content.

Questions

You can contact us at questions@packtpub.com if you are having a problem with any aspect of the book, and we will do our best to address it.

1
Exploring Test Doubles

"I never make stupid mistakes. Only very, very clever ones."

– John Peel

It is very difficult to find stupid mistakes, but it's even more daunting when you are trying to figure out the clever ones. Debugging an application to know how to fix a problem is very expensive and time-consuming. Automated unit tests provide an extremely effective mechanism for catching regressions, especially when combined with test-driven development; it creates a test safety net for the developers.

This chapter covers the concepts of unit testing, quality of unit tests, external dependencies, and test doubles.

The *Working with unit tests* section introduces you to test automation and describes the characteristics of a good unit test.

The *Understanding test doubles* section explores the concept of external dependency and provides examples of test doubles. The following test doubles are explored:

- Dummy objects
- Stubs
- Spies
- Mock objects
- Fake objects

Working with unit tests

A common understanding of *unit testing* is the testing of the smallest possible part of software, such as a single method, a small set of related methods, or a class.

In reality, we do not test methods; we test a logical unit and its behavior instead. Logical units can extend to a single method, to an entire class, or a collaboration of multiple classes.

For example, a standard calculator program can have an add method for adding two numbers. We can verify the add behavior by invoking the add method, or we can design the calculator program to have a simple calculate API, which can take two numbers and an operation (add, subtract, divide, and so on). Depending on the operand type (integer, double, and so on), the calculator may delegate the calculation to a collaborator class, such as a double calculator or a long calculator. We can still unit test the add behavior, but multiple classes (units) are involved now.

A unit test verifies an assumption about the behavior of the system. Unit tests should be automated to create a safety net so that the assumptions are verified continuously and a quick feedback can be provided if anything goes wrong.

The following are the benefits of test automation:

- **Behavior is continually verified**: We refactor code (change the internal structure of the code without affecting the behavior of the system) to improve the code's quality, such as maintainability, readability, or extensibility. We can refactor code with confidence if automated unit tests are running and giving feedback.

- **The side effects of code changes are detected immediately**: This is useful for a fragile, tightly-coupled system, where a change in one module breaks another module.

- **Saves time; no need for immediate regression testing**: Suppose that you are adding a scientific computational behavior to an existing calculator program and modifying the code; after every piece of change, you do a regression testing to verify the integrity of the system. Manual regression testing is tedious and time-consuming, but if you have an automated unit test suite, then you can delay the regression testing until the functionality is done. This is because the automated suite will inform you at every stage if you break an existing feature.

A unit test should exhibit the following characteristics:

- It should be automated, as explained in the preceding section.

- It should have a fast test execution. To be precise, a test should not take more than a few milliseconds to finish execution (they should be fast; the faster, the better). A system can have thousands of unit tests. If they take time to execute, then the overall test execution time will go up; as a result, no one will be interested in running the tests. It will impact the feedback cycle.

- A test should not depend on the result of another test or rather test execution order. Unit test frameworks can execute tests in any order. So, if a test depends on another test, then the test may fail any time and provide wrong feedback. You want tests to be standalone so that you can look at them and quickly see what they're actually testing, without having to understand the rest of the test code.

- A test should not depend on database access, file access, or any long running task. Rather, an appropriate test double should isolate the external dependencies.

- A test result should be consistent and time-and-location transparent. A test should not fail if it is executed at midnight, or it should not fail if it is executed in a different time zone.

- Tests should be meaningful. A class can have getter and setter methods; you should not write tests for the getters and setters because they should be tested in the process of other more meaningful tests. If they're not, then either you're not testing the functionality or your getters and setters aren't being used at all; so, they're pointless.

- Tests are system documentation. Tests should be readable and expressive; for example, a test that verifies the unauthorized access could be written as `testUnauthorizedAccess()` or rather `when_an_unauthorized_user_accesses_the_system_then_raises_secuirty_error()`. The latter is more readable and expresses the intent of the test.

- *Tests should be short* and *tests should not be treated as second-class citizens*. Code is refactored to improve the quality; similarly, unit tests should be refactored to improve the quality. A test class of 300 lines is not maintainable; we can rather create new test classes, move the tests to the new classes, and create a maintainable suite.

As per the preceding best practices, a test should be executed as fast as possible. Then what should you do if you need to test data access logic or file download code? Simple, do not include the tests in an automated test suite. Consider such tests as slow tests or integration tests. Otherwise, your continuous integration cycle will run for hours. Slow tests should still be automated. However, they may not run all the time, or rather they should be run out of the continuous integration feedback loop.

You cannot automate a unit test if your API class depends on *slow* external entities, such as data access objects or JNDI lookup. Then, you need test doubles to isolate the external dependencies and automate the unit test.

The next section covers test doubles.

Understanding test doubles

We all know about stunt doubles in movies. A stunt double or dummy is a trained replacement used for dangerous action sequences in movies, such as a fight sequence on the top of a burning train, jumping from an airplane, and so on, mainly fight scenes. Stunt doubles are used to protect the real actors, are used when the actor is not available, or when the actor has a contract to not get involved in stunts.

Similarly, sometimes it is not possible to unit test the code because of the unavailability of the collaborator objects, or the cost of interaction and instantiation of collaborators. For instance, when the code is dependent on database access, it is not possible to unit test the code unless the database is available, or when a piece of code needs to send information to a printer and the machine is not connected to a LAN. The primary reason for using doubles is to isolate the unit you are testing from the external dependencies.

Test doubles act as stunt doubles. They are a skilled replacement of the collaborator objects and allow you to unit test code in isolation from the original collaborator.

Gerard Meszaros coined the term **test doubles** in his book *xUNIT TEST PATTERNS, Addison-Wesley* — this book explores the various test doubles and sets the foundation for Mockito.

Test doubles can be created to impersonate collaborators and can be categorized into the types, as shown in the following diagram:

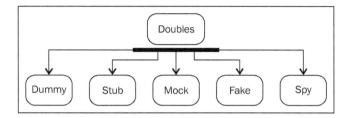

Using dummy objects

In movies, sometimes a double doesn't perform anything; they just appear on the screen. One such instance would be standing in a crowded place where the real actor cannot go, such as watching a soccer match or tennis match. It will be very risky for the real actor to go to a full house, but the movie's script needs it.

Likewise, a dummy object is passed as a mandatory parameter object. A dummy object is not directly used in the test or code under test, but it is required for the creation of another object required in the code under test. Dummy objects are analogous to null objects, but a dummy object is not used by the code under test. Null objects (as in the pattern) are used in the code under test and are actively interacted with, but they just produce zero behavior. If they weren't used, you'd just use an actual null value. The following steps describe the usage of dummy objects:

 In this book, we will write the code and JUnit tests in the Eclipse editor. You can download Eclipse from the following URL:

`https://www.eclopse.org/downloads`

1. Launch Eclipse and create a workspace, `\PacktPub\Mockito_3605OS\`; we'll refer to it as `<work_space>` in the next steps/chapters.

2. We'll create an examination grade system. The program will analyze the aggregate of all the subjects and determine the grade of a student. Create a Java project named `3605OS_TestDoubles`. Add an `enum` `Grades` field to represent a student's grades:

```
package com.packt.testdoubles.dummy;

public enum Grades {
    Excellent, VeryGood, Good, Average, Poor;
}
```

3. Create a Student class to uniquely identify a student:

```java
public class Student {

    private final String roleNumber;
    private final String name;

    public Student(String roleNumber, String name) {
        this.roleNumber = roleNumber;
        this.name = name;
    }

    //setters are ignored

}
```

4. Create a Marks class to represent the marks of a student:

```java
public class Marks {

    private final Student student;
    private final String subjectId;
    private final BigDecimal marks;

    public Marks(Student student, String subjectId,
        BigDecimal marks) {
        this.student = student;
        this.subjectId = subjectId;
        this.marks = marks;
    }
    //getters methods go here
}
```

Note that the Marks constructor accepts a Student object to represent the marks of a student. So, a Student object is needed to create a Marks object.

5. Create a `Teacher` class to generate a student's grades:

```java
public class Teacher {

    public Grades generateGrade(List<Marks> marksList) {

        BigDecimal aggregate = BigDecimal.ZERO;

        for (Marks mark : marksList) {
        aggregate = aggregate.add(mark.getMarks());
    }

        BigDecimal percentage = calculatePercent(aggregate,
          marksList.size());

        if (percentage.compareTo(new BigDecimal("90.00")) > 0) {
          return Grades.Excellent;
        }

        if (percentage.compareTo(new BigDecimal("75.00")) > 0) {
          return Grades.VeryGood;
        }

        if (percentage.compareTo(new BigDecimal("60.00")) > 0) {
          return Grades.Good;
        }

        if (percentage.compareTo(new BigDecimal("40.00")) > 0) {
          return Grades.Average;
        }

        return Grades.Poor;
    }

    private BigDecimal calculatePercent(BigDecimal aggregate,
      int numberOfSubjects) {
      BigDecimal percent = new BigDecimal(aggregate.
        doubleValue()/ numberOfSubjects);
      return percent;
    }
}
```

6. Create a `DummyStudent` class and extend the `Student` class. This is the dummy object. A dummy object will be the one that is not the real implementation and provides zero functionality or values. The `DummyStudent` class throws a runtime exception from all the methods. The following is the body of the `DummyStudent` class:

```
public class DummyStudent extends Student {

    protected DummyStudent() {
        super(null, null);
    }

    public String getRoleNumber() {
        throw new RuntimeException("Dummy student");
    }

    public String getName() {
        throw new RuntimeException("Dummy student");
    }

}
```

Note that the constructor passes `NULL` to the super constructor and throws a runtime exception from the `getRoleNumber()` and `getName()` methods.

7. Create a JUnit test to verify our assumption that when a student gets more than 75 percent (but less than 90 percent) in aggregate, then the teacher generates the grade as `VeryGood`, creates a `DummyStudent` object, and passes it as `Student` to the `Marks` constructor:

```
public class TeacherTest {

    @Test public void when_marks_above_seventy_five_percent_
        returns_very_good() {
    DummyStudent dummyStudent = new  DummyStudent();

    Marks inEnglish = new Marks(dummyStudent, "English002",
        new BigDecimal("81.00"));

    Marks inMath = new Marks(dummyStudent, "Math005", new
        BigDecimal("97.00"));

    Marks inHistory = new Marks(dummyStudent, "History007, new
        BigDecimal("79.00"));
```

```
List<Marks> marks = Arrays.asList(inHistory, inMaths,
  inEnglish);

Grades grade = new Teacher().generateGrade(marks);
assertEquals(Grades.VeryGood, grade);
  }
}
```

Note that a `DummyStudent` object is created and passed to all the three `Marks` objects, as the `Marks` constructor needs a `Student` object. This `dummyStudent` object is not used in the `Teacher` class or test method, but it is necessary for the `Marks` object. The `dummyStudent` object shown in the preceding example is a dummy object.

Working with stubs

A **stub** delivers indirect inputs to the caller when the stub's methods are called. Stubs are programmed only for the test scope. Stubs may record other information such as how many times they are invoked and so on.

Unit testing a happy path is relatively easier than testing an alternate path. For instance, suppose that you need to simulate a hardware failure or transaction timeout scenario in your unit test, or you need to replicate a concurrent money withdrawal for a joint account use case — these scenarios are not easy to imitate. Stubs help us to simulate these conditions. Stubs can also be programmed to return a hardcoded result; for example, a stubbed bank account object can return the account balance as $100.00.

The following steps demonstrate stubbing:

1. Launch Eclipse, open `<work_space>`, and go to the `3605OS_TestDoubles` project.

2. Create a `com.packt.testdoubles.stub` package and add a `CreateStudentResponse` class. This **Plain Old Java Object (POJO)** contains a `Student` object and an error message:

```
public class CreateStudentResponse {
  private final String errorMessage;
  private final Student student;

  public CreateStudentResponse(String errorMessage,
    Student student) {
    this.errorMessage = errorMessage;
    this.student = student;
  }
```

```
    public boolean isSuccess(){
      return null == errorMessage;
    }

    public String getErrorMessage() {
      return errorMessage;
    }
     public Student getStudent() {
     return student;
     }
  }
```

3. Create a StudentDAO interface and add a create() method to persist a student's information. The create () method returns the roll number of the new student or throws an SQLException error. The following is the interface definition:

```
public interface StudentDAO {
  public String create(String name, String className)
  throws SQLException;
}
```

4. Create an interface and implementation for the student's registration. The following service interface accepts a student's name and a class identifier and registers the student to a class. The create API returns a CreateStudentResponse. The response contains a Student object or an error message:

```
public interface StudentService {
  CreateStudentResponse create(String name, String
    studentOfclass);
}
```

The following is the service implementation:

```
public class StudentServiceImpl implements StudentService {
  private final StudentDAO studentDAO;

  public StudentServiceImpl(StudentDAO studentDAO) {
    this.studentDAO = studentDAO;
  }

  @Override public CreateStudentResponse create(String
    name, String studentOfclass) {
    CreateStudentResponse response = null;
    try{
```

```
    String roleNum= studentDAO.create (name,
      studentOfclass);
    response = new CreateStudentResponse(null, new
      Student(roleNum, name));
  }catch(SQLException e) {){
    response = new CreateStudentResponse
    ("SQLException"+e.getMessage(),  null);
  }catch (Exception e) {
    response = new CreateStudentResponse(e.getMessage(),
      null);
  }
  return response;
  }
}
```

 Note that the service implementation class delegates the `Student` object's creation task to the `StudentDAO` object. If anything goes wrong in the data access layer, then the DAO throws an `SQLException` error. The implementation class catches the exceptions and sets the error message to the response object.

5. How can you test the `SQLException` condition? Create a stub object and throw an exception. Whenever the `create` method is invoked on the stubbed DAO, the DAO throws an exception. The following `ConnectionTimedOutStudentDAOStub` class implements the `StudentDAO` interface and throws an `SQLException` error from the `create()` method:

```
package com.packt.testdoubles.stub;
import java.sql.SQLException;

public class ConnectionTimedOutStudentDAOStub implements
  StudentDAO {
  public String create(String name, String className)
  throws SQLException {
    throw new SQLException("DB connection timed out");
  }
}
```

This class should be created under the `test` source folder since the class is only used in tests.

6. Test the `SQLException` condition. Create a test class and pass the stubbed DAO to the service implementation. The following is the test code snippet:

```java
public class StudentServiceTest {
  private StudentService studentService;
  @Test
  public void when_connection_times_out_then_the_student
    _is_not_saved() {
    studentService = new StudentServiceImpl(new
      ConnectionTimedOutStudentDAOStub());
    String classNine = "IX";
    String johnSmith = "john Smith";
    CreateStudentResponse resp = studentService.
      create(johnSmith, classNine);
    assertFalse(resp.isSuccss());
  }
}
```

The error condition is stubbed and passed into the service implementation object. When the service implementation invokes the `create()` method on the stubbed DAO, it throws an `SQLException` error.

Stubs are very handy to impersonate error conditions and external dependencies (you can achieve the same thing with a mock; this is just one approach). Suppose you need to test a code that looks up a JNDI resource and asks the resource to return some value. You cannot look up a JNDI resource from a JUnit test; you can stub the JNDI lookup code and return a stubbed object that will give you a hardcoded value.

Exploring a test spy

A spy secretly obtains the information of a rival or someone very important. As the name suggests, a spy object spies on a real object. A spy is a variation of a stub, but instead of only setting the expectation, a spy records the method calls made to the collaborator. A spy can act as an indirect output of the unit under test and can also act as an audit log.

We'll create a spy object and examine its behavior; the following are the steps to create a spy object:

1. Launch Eclipse, open <work_space>, and go to the 36050S_TestDoubles project.

2. Create a `com.packt.testdoubles.spy` package and create a
   `StudentService` class. This class will act as a course register service.
   The following is the code for the `StudentService` class:

```java
public class StudentService {

    private Map<String, List<Student>> studentCouseMap = new
        HashMap<>();

    public void enrollToCourse(String courseName,Student
        student){
        List<Student> list = studentCouseMap.get(courseName);
        if (list == null) {
            list = new ArrayList<>();
        }

        if (!list.contains(student)) {
            list.add(student);
        }
        studentCouseMap.put(courseName, list);
    }

}
```

The `StudentService` class contains a map of the course names and students.
The `enrollToCourse` method looks up the map; if no student is enrolled,
then it creates a collection of students, adds the student to the collection, and
puts the collection back in the map. If a student has previously enrolled for
the course, then the map already contains a `Student` collection. So, it just
adds the new student to the `collection.students` list.

3. The `enrollToCourse` method is a `void` method and doesn't return a
   response. To verify that the `enrollToCourse` method was invoked with a
   specific set of parameters, we can create a spy object. The service will write to
   the spy log, and the spy will act as an indirect output for verification. Create
   a spy object to register method invocations. The following code gives the
   method invocation details:

```java
class MethodInvocation {

    private List<Object> params = new ArrayList<>();
    private Object returnedValue = null;
    private String method;

    public List<Object> getParams() {
```

```
      return params;
  }

  public MethodInvocation addParam(Object parm){
    getParams().add(parm);
    return this;
  }

  public Object getReturnedValue() {
    return returnedValue;
  }

  public MethodInvocation setReturnedValue(Object
    returnedValue) {
    this.returnedValue = returnedValue;
    return this;
  }

  public String getMethod() {
    return method;
  }

  public MethodInvocation setMethod(String method) {
   this.method = method;
    return this;
  }
}
```

The MethodInvocation class represents a method invocation: the method name, a parameter list, and a return value. Suppose a sum() method is invoked with two numbers and the method returns the sum of two numbers, then the MethodInvocation class will contain a method name as sum, a parameter list that will include the two numbers, and a return value that will contain the sum of the two numbers.

> Note that the setter methods return
> this(MethodInvocation). This coding approach is known as
> **builder pattern**. It helps to build an object in multiple steps. Java
> StringBuilder is an example of such a use:
>
>   StringBuilder builder = new StringBuilder();
>   builder.append("step1").append("step2")…

The following is the spy object snippet. It has a `registerCall`
method to log a method call instance. It has a map of strings and a
`List<MethodInvocation>` method. If a method is invoked 10 times, then
the map will contain the method name and a list of 10 `MethodInvocation`
objects. The spy object provides an invocation method that accepts a
method name and returns the method invocation count from the
`invocationMap` class:

```
public class StudentServiceSpy {
  private Map<String, List<MethodInvocation>> invocationMap
    = new HashMap<>();

  void registerCall(MethodInvocation invocation) {
    List<MethodInvocation> list = invocationMap.get
      (invocation.getMethod());
    if (list == null) {
      list = new ArrayList<>();
    }
    if (!list.contains(invocation)) {
      list.add(invocation);
    }

    invocationMap.put(invocation.getMethod(), list);
  }

  public int invocation(String methodName){
    List<MethodInvocation> list = invocationMap.get
      (methodName);
    if(list == null){
      return 0;
    }

    return list.size();
  }

  public MethodInvocation arguments(String methodName, int
    invocationIndex){
    List<MethodInvocation> list = invocationMap.get
      (methodName);
    if(list == null || (invocationIndex > list.size())){
      return null;
    }
    return list.get(invocationIndex-1);
  }
}
```

The `registerCall` method takes a `MethodInvocation` object and puts it in a map.

4. Modify the `StudentService` class to set a spy and log every method invocation to the spy object:

```
private StudentServiceSpy spy;
public void setSpy(StudentServiceSpy spy) {
  this.spy = spy;
}
public void enrollToCourse(String courseName, Student
    student) {
  MethodInvocation invocation = new MethodInvocation();
  invocation.addParam(courseName).addParam(student).
    setMethod("enrollToCourse");
  spy.registerCall(invocation);

  List<Student> list = studentCouseMap.get(courseName);
  if (list == null) {
    list = new ArrayList<>();
  }
  if (!list.contains(student)) {
    list.add(student);
  }

  studentCouseMap.put(courseName, list);
}
```

5. Write a test to examine the method invocation and arguments. The following JUnit test uses the spy object and verifies the method invocation:

```
public class StudentServiceTest {
  StudentService service = new StudentService();
  StudentServiceSpy spy = new StudentServiceSpy();

  @Test
  public void enrolls_students() throws Exception {
    //create student objects
    Student bob = new Student("001", "Robert Anthony");
    Student roy = new Student("002", "Roy Noon");
    //set spy
    service.setSpy(spy);

    //enroll Bob and Roy
    service.enrollToCourse("english", bob);
    service.enrollToCourse("history", roy);
```

```
//assert that the method was invoked twice
assertEquals(2, spy.invocation("enrollToCourse"));

//get the method arguments for the first call
List<Object> methodArguments = spy.arguments
  ("enrollToCourse", 1).getParams();

//get the method arguments for the 2nd call
List<Object> methodArguments2 = spy.arguments
  ("enrollToCourse", 2).getParams();

//verify that Bob was enrolled to English first
assertEquals("english", methodArguments.get(0));
assertEquals(bob, methodArguments.get(1));

//verify that Roy was enrolled to history
assertEquals("history", methodArguments2.get(0));
assertEquals(roy, methodArguments2.get(1));

        }

    }
```

Getting started with mock objects

A mock object is a combination of a spy and a stub. It acts as an indirect output for a code under test, such as a spy, and can also stub methods to return values or throw exceptions, like a stub. A mock object fails a test if an expected method is not invoked or if the parameters of the method don't match.

The following steps demonstrate the test failure scenario:

1. Launch Eclipse, open <work_space>, and go to the 3605OS_TestDoubles project.

2. Create a com.packt.testdoubles.mock package and a StudentService class. This class will act as a course register service. The following is the code for the StudentService class:

```
public class StudentService {

    private Map<String, List<Student>> studentCouseMap = new
    HashMap<>();

    public void enrollToCourse(String courseName, Student
        student){
        List<Student> list = studentCouseMap.get(courseName);
        if (list == null) {
          list = new ArrayList<>();
```

```
    }

    if (!list.contains(student)) {
      list.add(student);
    }

    studentCouseMap.put(courseName, list);
  }
}
```

3. Copy the `StudentServiceSpy` class and rename it as
    `StudentServiceMockObject`. Add a new method to verify
    the method invocations:

```
public void verify(String methodName, int
  numberOfInvocation){
  int actual = invocation(methodName);
  if(actual != numberOfInvocation){
    throw new IllegalStateException(methodName+" was
      expected ["+numberOfInvocation+"] times but
      actuallyactaully invoked["+actual+"] times");
  }
}
```

4. Modify the `StudentService` code to set the mock object, as we did in the
    spy example:

```
private StudentServiceMockObject mock;

public void setMock(StudentServiceMockObject mock) {
  this.mock = mock;
}
public void enrollToCourse(String courseName,Student
  student){
  MethodInvocation invocation = new MethodInvocation();

  invocation.addParam(courseName).addParam(student)
    .setMethod("enrollToCourse");

  mock.registerCall(invocation);
  ...//existing code
}
```

5. Create a test to verify the method invocation:

```
public class StudentServiceTest {
  StudentService service = new StudentService();
  StudentServiceMockObject mockObject = new
    StudentServiceMockObject();

  @Test
```

```java
public void enrolls_students() throws Exception {
  //create 2 students
  Student bob = new Student("001", "Robert Anthony");
  Student roy = new Student("002", "Roy Noon");

  //set mock/spy
  service.setMock(mockObject);

  //invoke method twice
  service.enrollToCourse("english", bob);
  service.enrollToCourse("history", roy);

  //assert that the method was invoked twice
  assertEquals(2,
  mockObject.invocation("enrollToCourse"));

  //verify wrong information, that enrollToCourse was
    //invoked once, but actually it is invoked twice
  mockObject.verify("enrollToCourse", 1);

}

}
```

6. Run the test; it will fail, and you will get a verification error. The following screenshot shows the JUnit failure output:

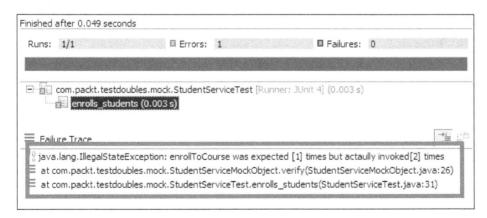

The Mockito framework provides an API for mocking objects. It uses proxy objects to verify the invocation and stub calls.

Implementing fake objects – simulators

A fake object is a test double with real logic (unlike stubs) and is much more simplified or cheaper in some way. We do not mock or stub a unit that we test; rather, the external dependencies of the unit are mocked or stubbed so that the output of the dependent objects can be controlled or observed from the tests. The fake object replaces the functionality of the real code that we want to test. Fakes are also dependencies, and don't mock via subclassing (which is generally always a bad idea; use composition instead). Fakes aren't just stubbed return values; they use some real logic.

A classic example is to use a database stub that always returns a fixed value from the DB, or a DB fake, which is an entirely in-memory nonpersistent database that's otherwise fully functional.

What does this mean? Why should you test a behavior that is unreal? Fake objects are extensively used in legacy code. The following are the reasons behind using a fake object:

- The real object cannot be instantiated, such as when the constructor reads a file, performs a JNDI lookup, and so on.
- The real object has slow methods; for example, a class might have a `calculate ()` method that needs to be unit tested, but the `calculate()` method calls a `load ()` method to retrieve data from the database. The `load()` method needs a real database, and it takes time to retrieve data, so we need to bypass the `load()` method to unit test the `calculate` behavior.

Fake objects are working implementations. Mostly, the fake class extends the original class, but it usually performs hacking, which makes it unsuitable for production.

The following steps demonstrate the utility of a fake object. We'll build a program to persist a student's information into a database. A data access object class will take a list of students and loop through the student's objects; if `roleNumber` is `null`, then it will insert/create a student, otherwise it will update the existing student's information. We'll unit test the data access object's behavior:

1. Launch Eclipse, open `<work_space>`, and go to the `36050S_TestDoubles` project.

2. Create a `com.packt.testdoubles.fake` package and create a `JdbcSupport` class. This class is responsible for database access, such as acquiring a connection, building a statement object, querying the database, updating the table, and so on. We'll hide the JDBC code and just expose a method for the batch update. The following are the class details:

```java
public class JdbcSupport {
  public int[] batchUpdate(String sql, List<Map<String,
    Object>> params){
    //original db access code is hidden
    return null;
  }
}
```

Check whether the `batchUpdate` method takes an SQL string and a list of objects to be persisted. It returns an array of integers. Each array index contains either `0` or `1`. If the value returned is `1`, it means that the database update is successful, and `0` means there is no update. So, if we pass only one `Student` object to update and if the update succeeds, then the array will contain only one integer as `1`; however, if it fails, then the array will contain `0`.

3. Create a `StudentDao` interface for the `Student` data access. The following is the interface snippet:

```java
public interface StudentDao {
  public void batchUpdate(List<Student> students);
}
```

4. Create an implementation of `StudentDao`. The following class represents the `StudentDao` implementation:

```java
public class StudentDaoImpl implements StudentDao {

  public StudentDaoImpl() {
  }

  @Override
  public void batchUpdate(List<Student> students) {

    List<Student> insertList = new ArrayList<>();
    List<Student> updateList = new ArrayList<>();

    for (Student student : students) {
      if (student.getRoleNumber() == null) {
        insertList.add(student);
      } else {
        updateList.add(student);
      }
    }

    int rowsInserted = 0;
```

```java
      int rowsUpdated = 0;

if (!insertList.isEmpty()) {
  List<Map<String, Object>> paramList = new
    ArrayList<>();
  for (Student std : insertList) {
    Map<String, Object> param = new HashMap<>();
    param.put("name", std.getName());
    paramList.add(param);
  }

  int[] rowCount = update("insert", paramList);
  rowsInserted = sum(rowCount);
}

if (!updateList.isEmpty()) {
  List<Map<String, Object>> paramList = new
    ArrayList<>();
  for (Student std : updateList) {
    Map<String, Object> param = new HashMap<>();
    param.put("roleId", std.getRoleNumber());
    param.put("name", std.getName());
    paramList.add(param);
  }

  int[] rowCount = update("update", paramList);
  rowsUpdated = sum(rowCount);
}

if (students.size() != (rowsInserted + rowsUpdated)) {
  throw new IllegalStateException("Database update error,
    expected "    + students.size() + " updates but
   actual " + (rowsInserted + rowsUpdated));
  }
}

public int[] update(String sql, List<Map<String,
  Object>> params) {
  return new JdbcSupport().batchUpdate(sql, params);
}

private int sum(int[] rows) {
  int sum = 0;
   for (int val : rows) {
     sum += val;
```

```
    }
    return sum;
  }


}
```

The `batchUpdate` method creates two lists; one for the new students and the other for the existing students. It loops through the `Student` list and populates the `insertList` and `udpateList` methods, depending on the `roleNumber` attribute. If `roleNumber` is NULL, then this implies a new student. It creates a SQL parameter map for each student and calls the `JdbcSupprt` class, and finally, checks the database update count.

5. We need to unit test the `batchUpdate` behavior, but the `update` method creates a new instance of `JdbcSupport` and calls the database. So, we cannot directly unit test the `batchUpdate()` method; it will take forever to finish. Our problem is the `update()` method; we'll separate the concern, extend the `StudentDaoImpl` class, and override the `update()` method. If we invoke `batchUpdate()` on the new object, then it will route the `update()` method call to the new overridden `update()` method.

    Create a `StudentDaoTest` unit test and a `TestableStudentDao` subclass:

```java
public class StudentDaoTest {
  class TestableStudentDao extends StudentDaoImpl{
    int[] valuesToReturn;
    int[] update(String sql, List<Map<String, Object>>
      params) {
      Integer count = sqlCount.get(sql);
      if(count == null){
        sqlCount.put(sql, params.size());
      }else{
        sqlCount.put(sql, count+params.size());
      }

      if (valuesToReturn != null) {
        return valuesToReturn;
      }


      return valuesToReturn;
    }
  }
}
```

Note that the update method doesn't make a database call; it returns a hardcoded integer array instead. From the test, we can set the expected behavior. Suppose we want to test a database update's fail behavior; here, we need to create an integer array of index 1, set its value to 0, such as int [] val = {0}, and set this array to valuesToReturn.

6. The following example demonstrates the failure scenario:

```java
public class StudentDaoTest {

    private TestableStudentDao dao;
    private Map<String, Integer> sqlCount = null;
    @Before
    public void setup() {
        dao = new TestableStudentDao();
        sqlCount = new HashMap<String, Integer>();
    }

    @Test(expected=IllegalStateException.class)
    public void when_row_count_does_not_match_then_rollbacks
        _tarnsaction(){
    List<Student>  students = new ArrayList<>();
    students.add(new Student(null, "Gautam Kohli"));

    int[] expect_update_fails_count = {0};
    dao.valuesToReturn = expect_update_fails_count;
    dao.batchUpdate(students);

    }
```

7. Check whether dao is instantiated with TestableStudentDao, then a new student object is created, and the valuesToReturn attribute of the fake object is set to {0}. In turn, the batchUpdate method will call the update method of TestableStudentDao, and this will return a database update count of 0. The batchUpdate() method will throw an exception for a count mismatch.

The following example demonstrates the new Student creation scenario:

```java
@Test
public void when_new_student_then_creates_student(){
    List<Student>  students = new ArrayList<>();
    students.add(new Student(null, "Gautam Kohli"));

    int[] expect_update_success = {1};
    dao.valuesToReturn = expect_update_success;
```

```
dao.batchUpdate(students);

    int actualInsertCount = sqlCount.get("insert");
    int expectedInsertCount = 1;
    assertEquals(expectedInsertCount, actualInsertCount);
}
```

Note that the valuesToReturn array is set to {1} and the Student object is created with a null roleNumber attribute.

8. The following example demonstrates the Student information update scenario:

```
@Test
public void when_existing_student_then_updates_
    student_successfully(){
    List<Student> students = new ArrayList<>();
    students.add(new Student("001", "Mark Leo"));
    int[] expect_update_success = {1};
    dao.valuesToReturn = expect_update_success;

    dao.batchUpdate(students);
    int actualUpdateCount = sqlCount.get("update");
    int expectedUpdate = 1;
    assertEquals(expectedUpdate, actualUpdateCount);
}
```

Note that the valuesToReturn array is set to {1} and the Student object is created with a roleNumber attribute.

9. The following example unit tests the create and update scenarios together. We will pass two students: one to update and one to create. So, update should return {1,1} for the existing students and {1} for the new student.

We cannot set this conditional value to the valuesToReturn array. We need to change the update method's logic to conditionally return the count, but we cannot break the existing tests. So, we'll check whether the valuesToReturn array is not null and then return valuesToReturn; otherwise, we will apply our new logic.

The following code snippet represents the conditional count logic:

```
class TestableStudentDao extends StudentDaoImpl {
    int[] valuesToReturn;
    int[] update(String sql, List<Map<String, Object>>
        params) {

        Integer count = sqlCount.get(sql);
```

```
      if(count == null){
        sqlCount.put(sql, params.size());
      }else{
        sqlCount.put(sql, count+params.size());
      }


      if (valuesToReturn != null) {
        return valuesToReturn;
      }

      int[] val = new int[params.size()];
      for (int i = 0; i < params.size(); i++) {
        val[i] = 1;
      }

      return val;
    }
}
```

When `valuesToReturn` is `null`, the `update` method creates an array of the `params` size and sets it as 1 for each index. So, when the update will be called with two students, the `update` method will return {1,1}.

The following test creates a student list of three students, two existing students with `roleNumbers` and one new student.

```
@Test
public void when_new_and_existing_students_then_creates
  _and_updates_students() {
  List<Student> students = new ArrayList<>();
  students.add(new Student("001", "Mark Joffe"));
  students.add(new Student(null, "John Villare"));
  students.add(new Student("002", "Maria Rubinho"));

  dao.batchUpdate(students);

}
```

The following screenshot shows the output of the JUnit execution:

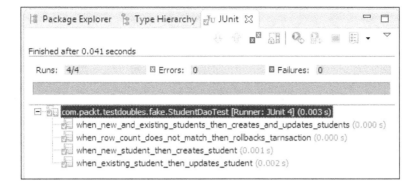

 Note that it took 0.041 seconds to execute four tests. This is interesting because it's something that you wouldn't easily get if you were using a real database.

Summary

This chapter covered the concept of automated unit tests, the characteristics of a good unit test, and explored tests doubles. It provided the examples of dummy objects, fake objects, stubs, mock objects, and spies.

By now, you will be able to identify the different test doubles and write unit tests using test doubles.

The next chapter, *Socializing with Mockito*, will focus on getting the reader quickly started with the Mockito framework.

2
Socializing with Mockito

"The significant problems that exist in the world today cannot be solved by the level of thinking that created them."

– Albert Einstein

This chapter distills the **Mockito** framework to its main core and provides technical examples. No previous knowledge of Mocking is necessary.

The following topics are covered in this chapter:

- Exploring Mockito
- Working with Mockito
- Understanding the Mockito architecture

The *Exploring Mockito* section covers the unit test qualities and significance of Mockito in unit testing.

The *Working with Mockito* section explicates the Mockito framework and covers the following topics:

- Stubbing method calls
- Verifying method invocation
- Matching arguments
- Answering method calls

The *Understanding the Mockito architecture* section explains the internal architecture of Mockito.

Exploring Mockito

Mockito is an open source mocking framework for Java. Mockito comes under the MIT license. The MIT license says that anybody can use the software free of charge and can use, copy, modify, merge, publish, distribute, and sell the software.

In *Chapter 1*, *Exploring Test Doubles*, we read about test doubles, spies, stubs, and mock objects. Test doubles replicate the external dependencies so that the code under test can interact with its external dependencies and allow you to isolate code from its dependencies to test them on a standalone basis. Mockito streamlines the creation and management of external dependencies and allows mock object creation, verification, stubbing, and spying on real objects. To learn more about Mockito, visit the following links:

- `https://github.com/mockito/mockito`
- `https://github.com/mockito/mockito/wiki`

Exploring unit test qualities

Writing clean, readable, and maintainable unit test cases (JUnit, TestNG) is an art; just like writing clean code. A well-written unit test can prevent maintenance nightmare and acts as a form of system documentation, but if not used carefully, it may produce meaningless boilerplate test cases.

Unit tests should adhere to a number of principles for readability, flexibility, and maintainability. This section elucidates the principles that we'll follow throughout this journey. The following are the principles:

- **Should be reliable**: A unit test should fail if, and only if, the production code is broken. If your test starts failing for some other reason, for example, if the database server is down or Internet connection is not available, it implies that your code is broken. However, in reality, your test is failing because of an external resource that is not a part of your code.

- **Unit tests should be automated**: The following are the benefits of test automation:

    ° **Assumptions are continually verified**: We refactor code (change the internal structure of the code without affecting the output of the system) to improve code quality in terms of maintainability, readability, or extensibility. We can refactor code with confidence if automated unit tests are running and giving feedback. We should not refactor code without proper test coverage.

- ° **Side effects are detected immediately**: This is useful for a fragile, tightly-coupled system when a change in one module breaks another module.

- ° **Saves time with no need for immediate manual regression testing**: If you are adding a scientific computation behavior to an existing calculator program and modifying the code, you need to do a regression to verify the integrity of the system after every piece of change. Regression testing is tedious and time consuming, but if you have an automated unit test suite, you can delay the regression testing until the functionality is done. This is because the automated suite will inform you at every stage if you break an existing feature.

- **Tests should be executed extremely fast**: This is because the tests can provide quick feedback. A test should not take more than a second to finish the execution. Your application can have thousands of tests. If they take hours to finish, every change you commit will have to wait for an hour to get the feedback, which is not acceptable.

- **Trouble-free setup and run**: Test setup should be simple. Unit tests should not require a DB connection or an Internet connection or delete a temp directory.

Mockito provides APIs to mock out the external dependencies and achieve the qualities mentioned here.

Realizing the significance of Mockito

Automated tests are a safety net. They run and notify if the system is broken so that the offending code can be fixed very quickly. If a test suite runs for an hour, the purpose of quick feedback is compromised.

Consider a development environment where every line of code changes (commits to the source control, for example, Git, SVN, or Rational ClearCase), triggers an automated test suite, and takes hours to complete. A developer has to wait for an hour or more to verify a new change until the test run is complete. This blocks the progress of the development.

A test may take time to execute or fail needlessly when your code exhibits testing-unfriendly behaviors or interacts with testing-unfriendly external objects.

The following are examples of testing-unfriendly behaviors:

- Acquiring a database connection and fetching/updating data
- Connecting to the Internet and downloading files
- Interacting with an SMTP server to send an e-mail
- Looking up JNDI objects
- Invoking a web service
- Performing I/O operations, such as printing a report

Do we really need a database connection or Internet connectivity to unit test a piece of code?

If the connection to a database is not possible or the stock price cannot be downloaded, the code cannot be tested and a few parts of the system remain untested. So, DB interaction or network connection is mandatory for unit testing some parts of the system. To unit test these parts, you need to isolate the testing of unfriendly objects, or technically, the external dependencies need to be mocked out (or faked).

Mockito plays a key role in mocking external dependencies. Mockito can be used to mock out a database connection or any external I/O behavior so that the actual logic can be unit tested and your code can interact with the mocked external objects.

Mocking provides the following benefits:

- **Unit test reliability**: You mock test unfriendly objects so that your test becomes reliable. They don't fail for any unavailable external object as you mock the external object.
- **Unit tests can be automated**: Mockito makes unit test configuration simple as the tests can mock external dependencies, such as a web service call or database access.
- **Extremely fast test execution**: Unit tests access mock objects, so delay in external service call or slow I/O operations can be isolated.

Working with Mockito

This section provides an overview of Mockito. Here is the official Mockito logo:

The following topics are covered in this section:

- Configuring Mockito
- Stubbing method calls
- Throwing exceptions
- Matching method arguments
- Verifying method calls

Download the latest Mockito binary ZIP folder from the following link and add it to the project dependency. The recommended channel for getting Mockito is Maven (or Gradle), or download it directly from the central Maven repository if you need to get the JAR files manually from either `http://central.maven.org/maven2/org/mockito/mockito-all/` or `http://central.maven.org/maven2/org/mockito/mockito-core/`.

As of April 2014, the latest Mockito version is 1.9.5.

Adding a Mockito dependency

The following steps describe how Mockito JAR files can be added as project dependency:

1. Extract the JAR files into a folder.
2. Launch Eclipse.
3. Create an Eclipse project named `3605OS_Socializing_with_Mockito`.
4. Go to the **Libraries** tab in the project's build path.

5. Click on the **Add External JARs...** button and browse to the Mockito JAR folder.

6. Select all the JAR files and click **OK**.

The following code snippet will add the Mockito dependency to a Maven project and download the JAR files from the central Maven repository (http://mvnrepository. com/artifact/org.mockito/mockito-core):

```
<dependency>
  <groupId>org.mockito</groupId>
  <artifactId>mockito-core</artifactId>
  <version>1.9.5</version>
  <scope>test</scope>
</dependency>
```

The following Gradle script snippet will add the Mockito dependency to a Gradle project:

```
testCompile 'org.mockito:mockito-core:1.9.5'
```

Stubbing method calls

This section demonstrates the mock objects with an example. The following jQuery table displays a list of countries:

This special table has numerous controls; you can sort by a column, either in descending or ascending order. The table displays selectable rows per page as a dropdown; you can change the number of records per page — you can choose **10**, **15**, **20**, **30**, or **50**. The table has a next page, previous page, first page, and last page widget. It has a refresh icon to load the latest dataset.

We need to create a controller class to accept the Ajax call from the jQuery table and return a country list. The Ajax request contains the requested page number, rows per page, sort order, sort column name, and search query. The controller needs to retrieve the country details from a database table and return only filtered countries as an Ajax response.

The following is the Ajax controller class:

```
@Controller
@Scope("session")
public class AjaxController {
  private final CountryDao countryDao;

  public AjaxController(CountryDao countryDao) {
    this.countryDao = countryDao;
  }

  @RequestMapping(value = "retrieveCountries", method =
    RequestMethod.POST)
  public @ResponseBody
  JsonDataWrapper<Country> retrieve(HttpServletRequest webRequest)
    {
    List<Country> countries = new ArrayList<Country  >();
    RetrieveCountryRequest request = RequestBuilder.build
      (webRequest);
    countries = countryDao.retrieve(request);
    Long startIndex = (request.getPage() - 1) *
      (request.getRowPerPage());
    int size = countries.size();
    Long endIndex = (startIndex + request.getRowPerPage()) > size
      ? size: (startIndex + request.getRowPerPage());
    if (startIndex < endIndex) {
      countries = countries.subList(startIndex.intValue(),
      endIndex.intValue());
    }

    JsonDataWrapper<Country> wrapper = new JsonDataWrapper
      <Country>(request.getPage(), size, countries);

    return wrapper;
  }

}
```

The `retrieve` method accepts an `HttpServletRequest` object and builds a database access request from this object. The following is the request's builder code:

```java
public class RequestBuilder {

   public static RetrieveCountryRequest build(HttpServlet
      RequestwebReq) {
      RetrieveCountryRequest request = new RetrieveCountryRequest();
      request.setPage(getLong(webReq.getParameter("page")));
      request.setRowPerPage(getInt(webReq.getParameter("rp")));
      request.setSortOrder(SortOrder.find(webReq.getParameter
         ("sortorder")));
      request.setSortname(SortColumn.find(webReq.getParameter
         ("sortname")));
      request.setSerachQuery(webReq.getParameter("qtype"));

      return request;
   }

   private static Integer getInt(String val) {
      Integer retVal = null;
      try {
         retVal = Integer.parseInt(val);
      } catch (Exception e) {
      }

   return retVal;
   }

   private static Long getLong(String val) {
      Long retVal = null;
      try {
         retVal = Long.parseLong(val);
      } catch (Exception e) {
      }
      return retVal;
   }
}
```

Finally, the `retrieve` method builds a `JsonDataWrapper` object from the country list and hands it over to the Ajax request as JSON data. The `@ResponseBody` annotation instructs the JSON response.

To unit test this class, we need to create an HttpServletRequest object, populate it with testable data, and then isolate the countryDao/database access call.

We'll use the Mockito framework to create a mock HttpServletRequest object and isolate the countryDao access call by stubbing the database call.

A mock object can be created with the help of a static method mock(). You need to invoke the Mockito.mock() method or static import Mockito's mock() method. The following is the syntax:

```java
import org.mockito.Mockito;
public class AjaxControllerTest {

  HttpServletRequest request;
  CountryDao countryDao;

  @Before
  public void setUp(){
    request = Mockito.mock(HttpServletRequest.class);
    countryDao = Mockito.mock(CountryDao.class);
  }
}
```

The following code snippet uses Java's static import construct:

```java
import static org.mockito.Mockito.mock;
public class AjaxControllerTest {

  HttpServletRequest request;
  CountryDao countryDao;

  @Before
  public void setUp(){
    request = mock(HttpServletRequest.class);
    countryDao = mock(CountryDao.class);
  }
}
```

 Static import in Java allows you to import static members and methods of Java classes and use them as if they are local variables or methods declared in the same class.

There's another way of mocking objects — using the @Mock annotation. But to work with the @Mock annotation, it is necessary to call MockitoAnnotations. initMocks(this) before using the mocks; or use MockitoJUnitRunner as a JUnit runner. We'll cover the annotation in depth in the next chapter. The following example is the syntax of mocking using the @Mock annotation:

```java
import org.junit.Before;
import org.mockito.Mock;
import org.mockito.MockitoAnnotations;
public class AjaxControllerTest {

  private @Mock HttpServletRequest request;
  private @Mock CountryDao countryDao;

  @Before
  public void setUp(){
    MockitoAnnotations.initMocks(this);
  }
}
```

The following is the syntax of the @Mock annotation using MockitoJUnitRunner:

```java
import org.junit.Before;
import org.junit.runner.RunWith;
import org.mockito.Mock;
import org.mockito.runners.MockitoJUnitRunner;

@RunWith(MockitoJUnitRunner.class)
public class AjaxControllerTest {

  private @Mock HttpServletRequest request;
  private @Mock CountryDao countryDao;

  @Before
  public void setUp() {
  }
}
```

Before we deep dive into the Mockito world, there are a few things to remember — Mockito cannot mock/spy the following things:

- Final classes
- Final methods
- Enums
- Static methods
- Private methods
- The hashCode() and equals() method
- Anonymous classes
- Primitive types

PowerMock has the capability to mock these constructs.

We read about stubs in *Chapter 1, Exploring Test Doubles.* The stubbing process defines the behavior of a mock method, such as what value should be returned or whether any exception should be thrown when the method is invoked.

The Mockito framework supports stubbing and allows us to return a given value when a specific method is called. It can be done using Mockito.when() along with thenReturn().

The following is the syntax for importing when:

```
import static org.mockito.Mockito.when;
```

The following test code stubs the retrieve method for CountryDao and returns an empty list. Finally, the stubbing is verified using the assertTrue method:

```
@Test
public void retrieves_empty_country_list() throws Exception {
  List<Country> list = new ArrayList<Country>();
  list.add(new Country());
  when(countryDao.retrieve(isA(RetrieveCountryRequest.class)))
    .thenReturn(emptyList);

  assertTrue(countryDao.retrieve(new RetrieveCountryRequest())
    .size() == 1);
}
```

The when() method represents the trigger — when to stub it. The following methods are used to represent a *trigger action* or *what to do* when the trigger is triggered.

- thenReturn (a value to be returned): This method returns a given value.

- thenThrow (a throwable to be thrown): This method throws a given exception.

- thenAnswer (Answer answer): In this method, unlike returning a hardcoded value, a dynamic, user-defined logic is executed; more like *fake* test doubles. Answer is an interface. Dynamic code logic is needed to implement the Answer interface.

- thenCallRealMethod (): This method calls the real method on the mock object/spy.

The thenReturn () method has a variant; it can either return a hardcoded value or can accept variable arguments of hardcoded values. What follows are the three ensuing variants:

- thenReturn (value)

- thenReturn (value, values...)

- thenReturn (value) . thenReturn (value2) . thenReturn (value3)

The thenReturn (value) variant returns the same hardcoded value for each method call, whereas when (mock.someMethod ()) .thenReturn (10,5,100) returns the following values:

- During the first invocation, mock.someMethod () returns 10

- During the second invocation, mock.someMethod () returns 5

- During the third invocation, mock.someMethod () returns 100

- During all the other invocations, mock.someMethod () returns 100

We'll use this style of mocking for HttpServletRequest. The following is the modified test:

```
@Test
public void retrieves_empty_country_list() throws Exception {
  when(request.getParameter(anyString())).thenReturn("1",
    "10",SortOrder.ASC.name(), SortColumn.iso.name());

  List<Country> countryList = new ArrayList<Country>();
  countryList.add(new Country());

  when(countryDao.retrieve(isA(RetrieveCountryRequest.class)))
    .thenReturn(countryList);
```

```
JsonDataWrapper<Country> response = ajaxController.retrieve
    (request);

assertEquals(1, response.getPage());
assertEquals(1, response.getTotal());
assertEquals(1, response.getRows().size());

}
```

The `RequestBuilder` class calls the `getParameter()` method of `HttpServletRequest` to fetch the request parameters. Sequentially, it calls `webReq.getParameter("page")`, `webReq.getParameter("rp")`, `webReq.getParameter("sortorder")`, and `webReq.getParameter("sortname")`.

In the test method, we stubbed the `getParameter` call with a variable argument `thenReturn` style.

We used two Mockito matchers, namely, `anyString` and `isA`. The `anyString()` matcher is used to stub the `getParameter` method. The `getParameter` method accepts a string argument, such as `webReq.getParameter("page")`. The `anyString` matcher is used as a generic argument matcher. This means, no matter what value is passed to the `getParameter` method, it will return a hardcoded value.

The `isA` matcher is used to stub the `retrieve` method of `CountryDao` to get the following:

* If the retrieve method is called with a `RetrieveCountryRequest` object, it will return the country list

In the next section, we'll discuss argument matchers.

Throwing exceptions

Unit tests are not meant only for happy path testing. We should test our code for failure conditions as well. Mockito provides an API to raise errors during testing. Suppose we are testing a flow where we compute some value and then send it to a printer; if the printer is not configured or a network error occurs or a page is not loaded, the system throws an exception. We can test this using Mockito's exception APIs.

How do we test exceptional conditions such as database access failure?

For this, Mockito provides a `thenThrow(Throwable)` method. This method tells the Mockito framework to throw a throwable (could be exception or error) when the stubbed method is invoked.

JUnit 4.0 provides a way to test exceptions using `@Test(expected=<exception>)`.

We'll stub the `countryDao` access call to throw an exception and assert the exception using `@Test(execpted=)`. If the test doesn't throw any exception, it will fail:

```
@Test(expected=RuntimeException.class)

public void when_system_throws_exception() {

    when(request.getParameter(anyString())).thenReturn("1", "10",
        SortOrder.DESC.name(), SortColumn.iso.name());


    when(countryDao.retrieve(isA(RetrieveCountryRequest.class))).
        thenThrow(new RuntimeException("Database failure"));


    JsonDataWrapper<Country> response = ajaxController.retrieve
        (request);

}
```

To throw an exception from a `void` method, use the following code syntax:

```
doThrow(exception).when(mock).voidmethod(arguments);
```

Checking and throwing `RuntimeException` is not recommended. Instead, we can use a specific exception in production code. In JUint 4, there exists an `ExpectedException` rule API for exception handling.

Using argument matchers

The argument matcher plays a key role in mocking. Mock objects return expected values, but when they need to return different values for different arguments, the argument matcher comes into play.

Suppose we have a method that takes a cricket player's name as an input and returns the number of runs as an output. We want to stub it and return `100` for the player `Sachin` and `10` for `xyz`. We have to use the argument matcher to stub this.

Mockito returns expected values when a method is stubbed. If the method takes arguments, the argument must match during the execution. For example, the `getValue(int someValue)` method is stubbed in the following way:

```
when(mockObject.getValue(1)).thenReturn(expected value);
```

Here, the getValue method is called with mockObject.getValue(100). The parameter doesn't match (it is expected that the method will be called with 1, but at runtime it encounters 100), so the mock object fails to return the expected value. It will return the default value of the return type. If the return type is int or short or long, it returns 0 for wrapper types such as integer and long. If it returns NULL for Boolean, it'll return false if the object is null and so on.

Mockito verifies argument values in natural Java style by using an object's equals() method. Sometimes, we use argument matchers when extra flexibility is required. Mockito provides built-in matchers, such as anyInt(), anyDouble(), anyString(), anyList(), and anyCollection(). More built-in matchers and examples of custom argument matchers / **hamcrest** matchers can be found at the following link:

https://github.com/mockito/mockito/blob/master/src/org/mockito/Matchers.java

> Examples of other matchers are isA(java.lang.Class<T> clazz), any(java.lang.Class<T> clazz), and eq(T) or eq(primitive value).

The isA matcher checks whether the passed object is an instance of the class type passed in the isA argument. The any(T) matcher also works in the same way.

Working with wildcard matchers

A test invokes a method on a code under test. When the invoked method creates a new object and passes that to a mock object, the test method doesn't have the reference of that new object. So the test cannot stub the mock method with a specific value, as the value is not available to the test method. In this context, we use the wildcard matchers.

In the following code snippet, an object is passed to a method and then a request object is created and passed to a service. Now, if we call someMethod from a test and service is a mocked object, we cannot stub callMethod from a test with a specific request, as the request object is local to someMethod.

```java
public void someMethod(Object obj){
    Request req = new Request();
    Req.setValue(obj);
    Response resp = service.callMethod(req);
}
```

In our jQuery example, we create a mock `HttpServletRequest` object and pass it to `AjaxController`. We have the control to stub the `HttpServletRequest` object, but inside the `retrieve` method, `AjaxController` creates a new instance of `RetrieveCountryRequest` and passes it to `CountryDao`. We don't have any control over the new instance of `RetrieveCountryRequest`, so we used a wildcard matcher `isA()` to stub the `retrieve` method of `CountryDao`.

While using argument matchers, all arguments have to be provided by matchers.

We're passing three arguments, and all of them are passed using matchers in the following manner:

```
verify(mock).someMethod(anyInt(), anyString(),
eq("third argument"));
```

The following example will fail because the first and the third argument are not passed using a matcher:

```
verify(mock).someMethod(1, anyString(), "third
argument");
```

Working with a custom ArgumentMatcher class

The `ArgumentMatcher` class allows us to create our own custom argument matchers. The `ArgumentMatcher` class is a hamcrest matcher with the predefined `describeTo()` method. Use the `Matchers.argThat(org.hamcrest.Matcher)` method and pass an instance of the hamcrest matcher. **Hamcrest** provides a utility matcher class, `org.hamcrest.CoreMatchers`. A few utility methods for `CoreMatchers` include `allOf`, `anyOf`, `both`, `either`, `describedAs`, `everyItem`, `is`, `isA`, `anything`, `hasItem`, `hasItems`, `equalTo`, `any`, `instanceOf`, `not`, `nullValue`, `notNullValue`, `sameInstance`, and `theInstance`. It also includes a few string methods such as `startsWith`, `endsWith`, and `containsString`. All these methods return a matcher.

Look at the usage of `assertThat` and explore the utility methods. The following section provides example of matchers. Let's start with `equalTo`. The `equalTo` matcher is equivalent to `assertEquals`.

Comparison matchers – equalTo, is, and not

Create a JUnit test, `AssertThatTest.java`, and static import `org.hamcrest.CoreMatchers.*;` in the following manner:

```
import static org.hamcrest.CoreMatchers.*;
import static org.junit.Assert.*;
```

```
import org.junit.Test;

public class AssertThatTest {

  @Test
  public void verify_Matcher() throws Exception {
    int age = 30;
    assertThat(age, equalTo(30));
    assertThat(age, is(30));

    assertThat(age, not(equalTo(33)));
    assertThat(age, is(not(33)));
  }
}
```

Set the `age` variable to `30` and then, like `assertEquals`, call `equalTo`, which is a matcher; `equalTo` takes a value. If the matcher value doesn't match the actual value, `assertThat` throws an `AssertionError`. Set the `age` variable value to `29` and rerun the test; the following error will occur:

```
java.lang.AssertionError:
Expected: <30>
     but: was <29>
  at org.hamcrest.MatcherAssert.assertThat(MatcherAssert.java:20)
  at org.junit.Assert.assertThat(Assert.java:865)
```

The `is` matcher takes a value and behaves similarly to `equalTo`. The `not` matcher takes a value or a matcher. In the preceding code, we used `assertThat(age, is(not(33)));`, which is nothing but `age is not 33` and more readable than assert methods.

Compound value matchers – either, both, anyOf, allOf, and not

In this section, we will use the `either`, `both`, `anyOf`, `allOf`, and `not` matchers. Add the following test to the `AssertThatTest.java` JUnit test:

```
@Test
public void verify_multiple_values() throws Exception {

  double marks = 100.00;
  assertThat(marks, either(is(100.00)).or(is(90.9)));

  assertThat(marks, both(not(99.99)).and(not(60.00)));
```

```
    assertThat(marks, anyOf(is(100.00),is(1.00),is(55.00),is(88.00),
      is(67.8)));

    assertThat(marks, not(anyOf(is(0.00),is(200.00))));

    assertThat(marks, not(allOf(is(1.00),is(100.00), is(30.00))));
  }
```

In the preceding example, a double variable mark is initialized with the value 100.00. This variable value is asserted with an either matcher.

Basically, using either, we can compare two values against an actual/calculated value. If any of them match, the assertion is passed. If none of them match, AssertionError is thrown.

The either(Matcher) takes a matcher and returns a CombinableEitherMatcher class. The CombinableEitherMatcher class has an or(Matcher other) method so that either and or can be combined:

```
or(Matcher other) is translated as
return (new CombinableMatcher(first)).or(other);-> finally to
new CombinableMatcher(new AnyOf(templatedListWith(other)));
```

Using both, we can compare two values against an actual/calculated value. If neither of them match, the assertion error is thrown. If both of them match, the assertion is passed.

A numeric value, like math score, cannot be equal to both 60 and 80. But we can negate the expression. If the math score is 80, using the both matcher, we can write the expression as assertThat (mathScore , both (not(60)). and(not (90))).

The anyOf matcher is more like either with multiple values. Using anyOf, we can compare multiple values against an actual/calculated value. If any of them match, the assertion is passed. If none of them match, the assertionError is thrown.

The allOf matcher is more like both with multiple values. Using allOf, we can compare multiple values against an actual/calculated value. If none of them match, the assertionError is thrown. Just like both, we can use allOf, along with not, to check that a value doesn't belong to a set.

In the preceding example, using allOf and not, we checked that the score is not 1 or 100 or 30.

We'll create a custom matcher for the jQuery table example.

The `CountryDao` access call accepts a request and returns a list of countries. The request contains the sort column name and the sort order. We can create a matcher to return the country list sorted in ascending order. The following is a custom matcher:

```
class SortByISOInAscendingOrderMatcher extends
ArgumentMatcher<RetrieveCountryRequest> {
  @Override
  public boolean matches(Object request) {
    if (request instanceof RetrieveCountryRequest) {
      SortOrder sortOrder = ((RetrieveCountryRequest) request)
        .getSortOrder();
      SortColumn col = ((RetrieveCountryRequest) request)
        .getSortname();

      return SortOrder.ASC.equals(sortOrder) && SortColumn
        .iso.equals(col);
    }
    return false;
  }
}
```

The preceding code extends the `ArgumentMatcher` class and overrides the `matches` method. The `matches` method checks the `RetrieveCountryRequest` request type, gets the `SortOrder` and `SortColumn` attributes from the request object, and finally, checks the `SortOrder` type. If the order is `ASC` and the column name is `ISO`, the match happens.

If you pass a `RetrieveCountryRequest` object with `SortOrder DESC` or `SortColumn ISO3`, the `matches` method returns `false` and the method is not stubbed. The following test method uses the custom matcher:

```
@Test
public void countryList_sortedBy_ISO_In_asc_order() {
  when(request.getParameter(anyString())).thenReturn("1", "10",
    SortOrder.ASC.name(), SortColumn.iso.name());

  Country argentina = new Country();
  argentina.setIso("AR");
  Country india = new Country();
  india.setIso("IN");
  Country usa = new Country();
  usa.setIso("US");

  List<Country> ascCountryList = new ArrayList<Country>();
  ascCountryList.add(argentina);
```

```
        ascCountryList.add(india);
        ascCountryList.add(usa);

        when(countryDao.retrieve(argThat(new SortByISOIn
          AscendingOrderMatcher()))).thenReturn(ascCountryList);

        JsonDataWrapper<Country> response = ajaxController.retrieve
          (request);
        assertEquals(ascCountryList, response.getRows());
    }
```

We stubbed the HttpServletRequest object to return SortOrder.ASC, populated a list, and stubbed the countryDao access call with argThat(new SortByISOInAscendingOrderMatcher()). If we stub the HttpServletRequest object to return a different sort order or sort column name, the test will fail.

Verifying method calls

To verify a redundant method invocation or if a stubbed method was not called but was important from the test perspective, we should manually verify the invocation. We need to use the static verify method.

Mock objects are used to stub external dependencies. We set an expectation and a mock object returns an expected value. In some conditions, a behavior/method of a mock object should not be invoked, or sometimes we may need to call the method N (a number) times. The verify method verifies the invocation of mock objects. Mockito does not automatically verify all stubbed calls; JMock does this automatically.

If a stubbed behavior should not be called, but is called due to bug in a code, the verify method flags the error (but we have to verify that manually). The void methods don't return a value; verify is very handy to test a void method's behavior (explained later).

The verify() method has an overloaded version, which takes VerificationMode (AtLeast, AtMost, Times, and so on) as an argument. The Times mode is a Mockito framework class of package, org.mockito.internal.verification, and it takes the integer argument, wantedNumberOfInvocations.

If `0` is passed to `Times`, it infers that the method will not be invoked in the testing path. We can pass `0` to `Times(0)` to make sure that the `sell` or `buy` methods are not invoked. If a negative number is passed to the `Times` constructor, Mockito throws `MockitoException - org.mockito.exceptions.base.MockitoException` and shows the **Negative value is not allowed here** error. The following methods are used in conjunction with `verify`:

- `times(int wantedNumberOfInvocations)`: This is invoked exactly N times. If the method is not invoked `wantedNumberOfInvocations` times, the test fails.

- `never()`: This is never called or is called as `times(0)`.

- `atLeastOnce()`: This is invoked at least once. It works fine if the method is invoked multiple times, but fails if the method is not invoked.

- `atLeast(int minNumberOfInvocations)`: This is called at least N times. It works fine if the method is invoked more than `minNumberOfInvocations` times, but fails if the method is not called `minNumberOfInvocations` times.

- `atMost(int maxNumberOfInvocations)`: This is called at the most N times. It fails if the method is called more than `minNumberOfInvocations` times.

- `only()`: This is used to verify that only one method is called on a mock. It fails if any other method is called on the mock object. In our example, if we use `verify(request, only()).getParameter(anyString());`, the test will fail with the following output:

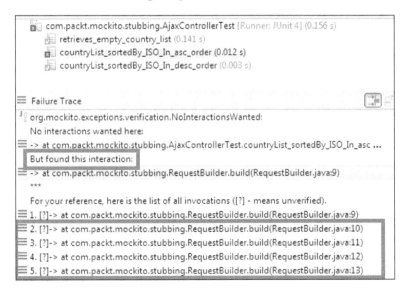

The test fails as it doesn't expect multiple calls to the `request.getParameter()` method.

- `timeout(int millis)`: This is specified in a time range.

Verifying zero and no-more interactions

The `verifyZeroInteractions (object, mocks)` method verifies that no interactions happened on the given mocks. The following test code directly calls the `verifyZeroInteractions` and passes the two mock objects. Since no methods are invoked on the mock objects, the test passes.

```
@Test public void verify_zero_interaction() {
  verifyZeroInteractions(request,countryDao);
}
```

This is useful if your code depends on two or more collaborators. For a given input, only one collaborator should handle the request while others should just ignore the request.

The `verifyNoMoreInteractions (Object, mocks)` method checks if any of the given mocks have any unverified interaction. We can use this method after verifying a mock method to make sure that nothing else was invoked on the mock.

This is generally not a good practice as it makes your tests overly brittle and you end up testing more than just what you care about. The following test code demonstrates the `verifyNoMoreInteractions` method:

```
@Test public void verify_nomore_interaction() {
  request.getParameter("page");
  request.getContextPath();

  verify(request).getParameter(anyString());
  //this will fail getContextPath() is not verified
  verifyNoMoreInteractions(request);
}
```

The following is the JUnit output. The test fails as the `getContextPath()` method was not verified even though the `getParameter()` method was verified. So the test considered the `getContextPath()` method invocation as a coding bug and `verifyNoMoreInteractions` raised the error.

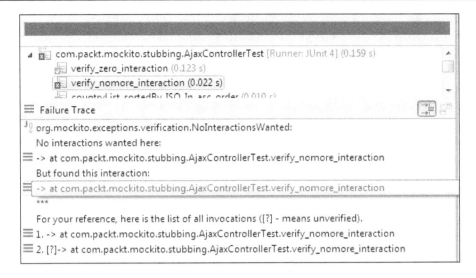

Answering method calls

Stubbed methods return a hardcoded value but cannot return a dynamic on-the-fly result. Mockito framework offers callbacks to compute on-the-fly results.

Mockito allows stubbing with the generic `Answer` interface; this is a callback. When a stubbed method on a mock object is invoked, the `answer(InvocationOnMock invocation)` method of the `Answer` object is called. This `Answer` object's `answer()` method returns the actual object. The syntax is similar to `thenReturn()` and `thenThrow()`:

```
when(mock.someMethod()).thenAnswer(new Answer() {…});
```

Alternatively, we can also use the following syntax:

```
when(mock.someMethod()).then(answer);
```

The `Answer` interface is defined as follows:

```
public interface Answer<T> {
  T answer(InvocationOnMock invocation) throws Throwable;
}
```

The `InvocationOnMock` argument is an important part of a callback. It gives you the arguments passed to the method and the mock object as well. The following methods of `InvocationOnMock` are used to get the arguments and the mock object:

```
Object[] args = invocation.getArguments();
Object mock = invocation.getMock();
```

The `retrieve` method of `CountryDao` is stubbed. We'll create an `answer` object to dynamically sort the country list based on the input sort order.

In test class, create a list for storing countries, and in the `setUp` method, populate the list with countries. The following is the changed test code:

```java
List<Country> countries;

@Before
public void setUp() {
    ajaxController = new AjaxController(countryDao);
    countries = new ArrayList<Country>();
    countries.add(create("Argentina", "AR", "32"));
    countries.add(create("USA", "US", "01"));
    countries.add(create("Brazil", "BR", "05"));
    countries.add(create("India", "IN", "91"));
}
```

Write a new `Answer` class to sort the countries list based on the user input. The following example is the custom `Answer` class:

```java
class SortAnswer implements Answer<Object> {
@Override
public Object answer(InvocationOnMock invocation) throws
    Throwable {
    RetrieveCountryRequest request = (RetrieveCountryRequest)
        invocation.getArguments()[0];
    final int order = request.getSortOrder().equals(SortOrder.ASC)
        ? 1: -1;
    final SortColumn col = request.getSortname();
    Collections.sort(countries, new Comparator<Country>() {
        public int compare(Country arg0, Country arg1) {
            if (SortColumn.countryCode.equals(col))
            return order * arg0.getCountryCode().compareTo
                (arg1.getCountryCode());

            if (SortColumn.iso.equals(col))
            return order * arg0.getIso().compareTo(arg1.getIso());
```

```
            return order * arg0.getName().compareTo(arg1.getName());
        }
    });

    return countries;
    }
}
```

The `answer` method gets the request object and sorts the countries list based on the `SortOrder` and `SortColumn` attributes. The following test verifies the ascending and descending sorting:

```
@Test
public void sorting_asc_on_iso() {
    when(request.getParameter(anyString())).thenReturn("1", "10",
        SortOrder.ASC.name(),    SortColumn.iso.name());


    when(countryDao.retrieve(isA(RetrieveCountryRequest.class)))
        .thenAnswer(new SortAnswer());

    JsonDataWrapper<Country> response = ajaxController.
        retrieve(request);
    assertEquals("AR", response.getRows().get(0).getIso());
    assertEquals("BR", response.getRows().get(1).getIso());
    assertEquals("IN", response.getRows().get(2).getIso());
    assertEquals("US", response.getRows().get(3).getIso());
}

@Test
public void sorting_desc_on_iso() {
    when(request.getParameter(anyString())).thenReturn("1",
        "10",SortOrder.DESC.name(), SortColumn.iso.name());

    when(countryDao.retrieve(isA(RetrieveCountryRequest.class)))
        .thenAnswer(new SortAnswer());

    JsonDataWrapper<Country> response = ajaxController.retrieve
        (request);
    assertEquals("AR", response.getRows().get(3).getIso());
    assertEquals("BR", response.getRows().get(2).getIso());
    assertEquals("IN", response.getRows().get(1).getIso());
    assertEquals("US", response.getRows().get(0).getIso());

}
```

Understanding the Mockito architecture

Mockito applies the proxy design pattern to create mock objects. For concrete classes, Mockito internally uses CGLib to create proxy stubs. CGLib is used to generate dynamic proxy objects and intercept field access. The following URL talks about CGLib:

```
https://github.com/cglib/cglib
```

The following sequence diagram depicts the call sequence. The `ClassImposterizer` class is a singleton class. This class has a `createProxyClass` method for generating a source using CGLib. Finally, it uses reflection to create an instance of the proxy class. Method calls are stubbed using the callback API of `MethodInterceptor`.

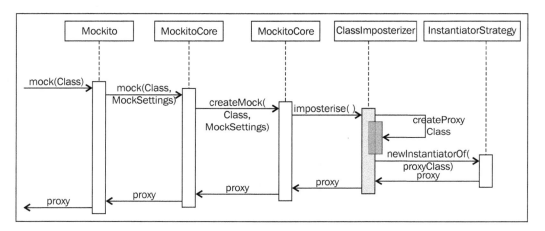

The `MethodInterceptor` class acts as a Java reflection class, `java.lang.reflect.InvocationHandler`. Any method call on a mock object (proxy) is handled by a `MethodInterceptor` instance.

We'll create a custom mocking framework to handle external dependencies. We'll use the Java reflection framework's dynamic proxy object-creation API. The `java.lang.reflect.Proxy` method provides a `Proxy.newProxyInstance(ClassLoader, Class, InvocationHandler)` API to create dynamic proxy objects. The `InvocationHandler` interface has the following signature:

```java
public interface InvocationHandler {

    public abstract Object invoke(Object obj, Method method,
        Object aobj[])  throws Throwable;
}
```

All method calls to a proxy object are redirected to the `invoke` method.

Create a class `OurMockito` for handling dynamic proxies. The following is the `OurMockito` class definition. It implements the `InvocationHandler` interface, provides an implementation of the `invoke()` method, and provides three static `mock` methods and two `stub` methods.

```
public class OurMockito implements InvocationHandler {
    private static Map<String, Object> stubMap = new HashMap<String,
        Object>();
    private static Map<String, Exception> excepMap = new
        HashMap<String, Exception>();

    @Override
    public Object invoke(Object proxy, Method method, Object[] args)
        throws Throwable {

        String methodName = method.getName();
        if (Modifier.isFinal(method.getModifiers()) ||
            Modifier.isPrivate(method.getModifiers()) ||
            Modifier.isStatic(method.getModifiers())) {
            throw new RuntimeException("You naughty developer mocking
                a private, static or final method "+ methodName);
        }

        if (excepMap.containsKey(methodName)) {
            Exception excep = excepMap.get(methodName);
            throw excep;
        }

        if (stubMap.containsKey(methodName)) {
            return stubMap.get(methodName);
        }

        return null;
    }
```

The `mock()` method takes a `java.lang.Class`, creates a proxy object of the class, and passes an instance of `OurMockito()` as `InvocationHandler`. The following is the body of the `mock()` method:

```
public static Object mock(Class aClass) {
    Object newProxyInstance = Proxy.newProxyInstance
        (OurMockito.class.getClassLoader(), new  Class[] { aClass
        },new OurMockito());
    return newProxyInstance;
}
```

The two overloaded stub methods are as follows:

```
public static void stub(Object stubOn, String methodName, Object
    stubbedValue) {
  stubMap.put(methodName, stubbedValue);
}

public static void stub(Object stubOn,String methodName,
    Exception excep) {
  if (excep != null) {
    excepMap.put(methodName, excep);
  }
}
}
```

The `mock` method uses the proxy class to generate a proxy object. The `stub(Object stubOn, String methodName, Object stubbedValue)` method allows a method call return value to stub. The `stub(Object stubOn,String methodName, Exception excep)` method allows an exception to be thrown on a method call to check the negative testing path. The stub methods populate two hashmaps for storing the stubbed values/exceptions. The reflection API delegates the method calls (on proxy objects) to `InvocationHandler`. The `invoke` method in the `OurMockito` class handles the method calls. The `invoke` method looks up the method name in the exception map. If the method was stubbed for throwing an exception, the exception is thrown; otherwise, the method stub map is looked up for returning a stubbed value.

Create an interface to represent an external dependency. The following is the class:

```
public interface ExternalService {
  public String concat(String arg1, String arg2);
  public void someStrangeOperation(Object obj);
  public int divide(int a, int b);
}
```

Now create a test class to verify the mocking capability. The following is the class:

```
public class OurMockTest {

  ExternalService externalService = (ExternalService)OurMockito
    .mock(ExternalService.class);

  @Test
  public void stubbing_method() throws Exception {
    OurMockito.stub(externalService, "concat", "dummy");
    String returned = externalService.concat(null, null);
```

```
      assertEquals("dummy", returned);
    }

    @Test
    public void stubbing_error_conditions() throws Exception {
      OurMockito.stub(externalService, "divide", 0);
      int returned = externalService.divide(0, 0);
      assertEquals(0, returned);
    }

    @Test
    public void stubbing_exception() throws Exception {
      OurMockito.stub(externalService, "someStrangeOperation", new
        RuntimeException("Just blow this up!"));
      externalService.someStrangeOperation(null);
    }
  }
```

The `ExternalService` method is mocked using following construct:

```
ExternalService externalService = (ExternalService)OurMockito.mock
  (ExternalService.class);
```

The `concat` method is stubbed to return a string `"dummy"`, the divide method is stubbed to return a hardcoded integer `0`, and the `someStrangeOperation` method is stubbed to throw a `RuntimeException`. The following is the JUnit output:

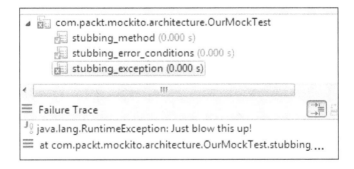

 Note that the third test throws the `RuntimeException` (`"Just blow this up!"`).

Summary

This chapter covered the Mockito overview, unit test qualities, and the significance of Mockito in unit testing. It explained and provided examples of stubbing, answering, throwing exceptions, argument matcher, and method call verification. It also covered the Mockito architecture.

By now, you should be able to verify method calls, stub methods, and throw exceptions using the Mockito framework.

The next chapter, *Accelerating Mockito*, focuses on advanced Mockito topics.

3
Accelerating Mockito

"Any sufficiently advanced technology is indistinguishable from magic."

– Arthur C. Clarke

This chapter explores the advanced topics of the **Mockito** framework. Using Mockito's advanced features, we can stub out void methods, capture arguments passed to the stubbed methods and assert the argument values, verify the invocation order to check that the collaborators are accessed in proper order, spy a real object and set expectation on the spy object in the legacy code, and change mocking behavior.

The following topics are covered in this chapter:

- Void methods
- Annotations
- Argument captor
- Verifying an invocation order
- Spying an object
- Changing default Mockito settings
- Resetting mock objects
- Inline stubbing
- Mock details

Learning advanced Mockito features

Chapter 2, *Socializing with Mockito*, explained the external dependencies and provided examples of basic Mockito features, such as stubbing method calls, throwing exceptions, matching arguments, verifying method invocations, and answering method calls.

Mockito provides a fluent API for mocking Java objects. It offers a collection of advanced features for advanced users. This section deals with the advanced Mockito features and answers several questions, such as how to change the Mockito settings to return smart null values instead of default return types, how to reset a mock object to clear all previous information, how to determine whether an object is a spy or a mock, and how to capture arguments passed to a mock object and verify the values.

The following sections cover the advanced Mockito APIs.

Working with void methods

Unit testing void methods is difficult. Conventional unit tests prepare data, pass values to a method, and then assert the return type to verify the behavior of the code. But when a method doesn't return a value but only changes the internal state of the object under test, it becomes difficult to decide what to assert. Conventional unit tests work with direct input and output, but void methods need to work with indirect output.

In this section, we'll examine a legacy servlet code and write unit test for the legacy code. To unit test a servlet code, you need the `Servlet-apiXX.jar`, JUnit JAR file, and the `Mockito` JAR file. To download `servlet-api.<version number>.jar`, you can visit the Oracle URL at `http://www.oracle.com/technetwork/java/javasebusiness/downloads/java-archive-downloads-eeplat-419426.html`, and we already have the JUnit and Mockito JAR files. On the other hand, you can download the code and associated JAR files for this chapter from the Packt website.

The following servlet code acts as a front controller. It intercepts all the web requests and delegates these requests to appropriate resources. The `DemoController` servlet extends from `HttpServlet` and has a dependency on a `LoginController` class. The constructor creates an instance of `LoginController`, as shown in the following code:

```
@WebServlet("/DemoController")
public class DemoController extends HttpServlet {
  private LoginController loginController;
  public DemoController() {
    loginController = new LoginController( new LDAPManagerImpl());
  }
}
```

The doPost() and doGet() methods are inherited from HttpServlet. The doPost() method intercepts the HTTP POST requests, and delegates calls to the doGet() method.

```
protected void doPost(HttpServletRequest request, HttpServlet
  Response response) throws ServletException, IOException {
  doGet(request, response);
}
```

The doGet() method intercepts all the HTTP GET requests, and depending on the request context URL, it routes the requests to appropriate handlers. Initially, the login.jsp page is opened for user login. On submission of the **Login** form, the /logon.do action is taken. The loginController class handles the /logon.do request, and all other requests are routed to the error page. The following is the body of the doGet() method:

```
protected void doGet(HttpServletRequest req, HttpServletResponse
res) throws ServletException, IOException {
  String urlContext = req.getServletPath();
  if(urlContext.equals("/")) {
    req.getRequestDispatcher("login.jsp").forward(req, res);
  }else if(urlContext.equals("/logon.do")) {
    loginController.process(req, res);
  }else {
    req.setAttribute("error", "Invalid request path
      '"+urlContext+"'");
    req.getRequestDispatcher("error.jsp").forward(req, res);
  }
}
```

The LoginController class has a dependency on LDAPManager for user validation. This class handles the login request, retrieves the username and encrypted password from the HTTP request, and asks the LDAPManager to validate whether the user exists or not. The following is the LoginController class:

```
public class LoginController {
  private final LDAPManager ldapManager;

  public LoginController(LDAPManager ldapMngr) {
    this.ldapManager = ldapMngr;
  }
}
```

The `process()` method delegates user validation to `LDAPManager` and if the user is valid, then it creates a new session, puts the user information to the session, and routes the user to the home page. However, if the username or password is invalid, it forwards the request back to the login page.

```
public void process(HttpServletRequest req, HttpServletResponse
  res) throws ServletException, IOException {
  String userName = req.getParameter("userName");
  String encrypterPassword = req.getParameter
    ("encrypterPassword");
  if (ldapManager.isValidUser(userName, encrypterPassword)) {
    req.getSession(true).setAttribute("user", userName);
    req.getRequestDispatcher("home.jsp").forward(req, res);
  } else {
    req.setAttribute("error", "Invalid user name or password");
    req.getRequestDispatcher("login.jsp").forward(req, res);
  }
}
```

The `process()` method doesn't return any value, but validates user login, and on successful login, it routes the user to the home page. How can we unit test this behavior? We can verify that the `isValidUser()` method of `LDAPManager` is invoked, then check that the username is put in the session, and confirm that the request is dispatched to the `home.jsp` page.

We learned about the mocking object and verifying method invocation using the `verify()` method in *Chapter 2, Socializing with Mockito*. Here, we'll create a mock `HttpServletRequest`, `HttpServletResponse`, and an `LDAPManager` and verify that the actions are taken. We'll stub the `isValidUser` method of `LDAPManager` to return `true` to unit test the successful user login and return `false` to unit test the invalid login scenario. The following is the JUnit setup for the `LoginController` class:

```
package com.packt.mockito.advanced.voidmethods;
import javax.servlet.http.HttpServletRequest;
import javax.servlet.http.HttpServletResponse;
import org.junit.Before;
import org.junit.Test;
import org.mockito.Mock;
import org.mockito.MockitoAnnotations;

public class LoginControllerTest {
  private LoginController controller;
  private @Mock HttpServletRequest request;
  private @Mock HttpServletResponse response;
  private @Mock LDAPManager ldapManager;
```

```
@Before
public void beforeEveryTest(){
  MockitoAnnotations.initMocks(this);
    controller = new LoginController(ldapManager);
}

@Test
public void when_valid_user_credentials_for_login_Then_
  routes_to_home_page(){
}
@Test
public void when_invalid_user_credentials_Then_
  routes_to_login_page(){
}
}
```

Mock objects are instantiated by the MockitoAnnotations.initMocks(this) instance in the beforeEveryTest method. Two empty test methods are created for unit testing the valid and invalid login, and the sanity checking of the mock objects creation. We'll start with the happy path. Modify the when_valid_user_credentials_for_login_Then_routes_to_home_page() test, and then we'll modify the when_invalid_user_credentials_Then_routes_to_login_page test.

After successful login, the process() method creates a user session, puts the user information to the session, and then dispatches the request. Hence, for this, we need to create a mock HttpSession object and a RequestDispatcher object:

```
@Mock HttpSession session;
@Mock RequestDispatcher dispatcher;
```

We modify the happy path test to verify successful login. Happy path unit tests can verify the most obvious things, such as when a valid user ID and password is passed, the user can login; but when we test complicated business conditions, such as an invalid password or an expired password, we call it the alternate path or sad path. The following is the modified test:

```
@Test
public void when_valid_user_credentials_for_login_Then_
  routes_to_home_page() throws Exception{
  verify(ldapManager).isValidUser(anyString(),anyStrin());
  verify(request).getSession(true);
  verify(session).setAttribute(anyString(), anyString());
  verify(request).getRequestDispatcher(eq("home.jsp"));
  verify(dispatcher).forward(request, response);
}
```

We are verifying a successful login that requires a user session to be created, a session attribute to be set, a request dispatcher object to be created for the home page ("home.jsp"), and the request dispatcher to be forwarded to the home page. The JUnit test verifies that things are set up and executed sequentially. Similarly, modify the other test to unit test the invalid login. The following is the modified test:

```
@Test
public void when_invalid_user_credentials_Then_routes_to_
    login_page() throws Exception{
    verify(request).getRequestDispatcher(eq("login.jsp"));
    verify(dispatcher).forward(request, response);
}
```

The following output is shown in the Eclipse JUnit runner when we run the unit tests:

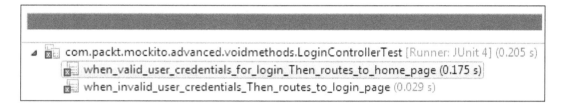

We need to invoke the process() method and modify the first test to stub LDAPManager to return true in order to simulate a successful login. The following is the modified test:

```
@Test
public void when_valid_user_credentials_for_login_Then_routes
    _to_home_page() throws Exception{
    when(ldapManager.isValidUser(anyString(), anyString()))
        .thenReturn(true);
    when(request.getSession(true)).thenReturn(session);
    when(request.getRequestDispatcher(anyString()))
        .thenReturn(dispatcher);
    when(request.getParameter(anyString()))
        .thenReturn("user","pwd");

    controller.process(request, response);

    verify(request).getSession(true);
    verify(session).setAttribute(anyString(), anyString());
    verify(request).getRequestDispatcher(eq("home.jsp"));
    verify(dispatcher).forward(request, response);
}
```

The isValidUser method of the ldapManager is stubbed to return true, request. getSession() is stubbed to return a mock HttpSession object, request. getRequestDispatcher() is stubbed to return a mock RequestDispatcher, and finally, the request.getParameter method is stubbed to return "user" and then "pwd". When we run the tests again, the first test passes! The following is the test output:

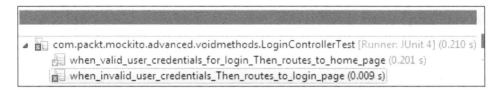

We must modify the second test to stub the isValidUser method to return false, stub the request.getRequestDispatcher() to return a mock RequestDispatcher, and finally, stub the request.getParameter method to return "user" and then "pwd". The following is the modified test:

```
@Test
public void when_invalid_user_credentials_Then_routes_to
  _login_page() throws Exception{
  when(ldapManager.isValidUser(anyString(), anyString()))
    .thenReturn(false);
  when(request.getRequestDispatcher(anyString()))
    .thenReturn(dispatcher);
  when(request.getParameter(anyString()))
    .thenReturn("user","pwd");

  controller.process(request, response);

  verify(request).getRequestDispatcher(eq("login.jsp"));
  verify(dispatcher).forward(request, response);
}
```

When we run the tests, we get a green bar as shown in the following screenshot:

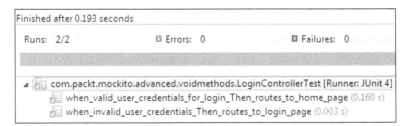

We learned how to unit test void methods. Revisit the tests; you will find duplicate code in the test methods, such as stubbing the getParameter() method or stubbing the getRequestDispatcher() method. You can move the stubbing calls to the beforeEveryTest method to clean the test code.

The following section explores the concept of exception handling for void methods.

Throwing exceptions from void methods

In the preceding example, the LoginController class calls the LDAPManager for user validation. The web application fails if the LDAPManager throws an exception. The DemoController servlet is the gateway; it should handle any unwanted exceptions and show a proper error message to the user. We have to find a mechanism to handle exceptions.

We'll create a unit test for the DemoController servlet. To recreate an exceptional condition, we have to stub the LoginController class to throw an exception, but the problem is the DemoController constructor. The constructor instantiates the LoginController class, so we cannot mock the controller. We can refactor the DemoController constructor to pass a mock instant of the LoginController class. There are several ways to achieve this; for now, we'll add a constructor to pass the mocked LoginController class. We cannot remove the default constructor, otherwise the servlet container will fail to instantiate the servlet. Servlets run in a container and the container maintains the servlet's lifecycle. The container invokes the default constructor to instantiate a servlet instance. If we remove the default constructor, the container will fail to create the servlet. The following is the modified code:

```
@WebServlet("/DemoController")
public class DemoController extends HttpServlet {
  private final LoginController loginController;

  public DemoController(LoginController loginController) {
    this.loginController = loginController;
  }
  public DemoController() {
    loginController = new LoginController(new LDAPManagerImpl()) ;
  }
}
```

The following is the empty unit test for the `DemoController` constructor:

```
public class DemoControllerTest {
  DemoController controller;
  @Mock LoginController loginController;

  @Before  public void beforeEveryTest(){
    MockitoAnnotations.initMocks(this);
    controller = new DemoController(loginController);
  }
}
```

We'll modify the code to handle the exceptions and route the request to an error page. After catching the exception, the servlet will dispatch the request to the error page. So we need to create a mock `HttpServletRequest` object, an `HttpServletResponse` object, and a `RequestDispatcher` object:

```
@Mock HttpServletRequest request;
@Mock HttpServletResponse response;
@Mock RequestDispatcher dispatcher;
```

Add the following test to simulate the scenario:

```
@Test
public void when_subsystem_throws_exception_Then_routes_to_
  error_page_() throws Exception {

  verify(request).getRequestDispatcher(eq("error.jsp"));
  verify(dispatcher).forward(request, response);
}
```

We are verifying the request dispatcher creation for the `error.jsp` error page. The `LoginController` class needs to throw an exception. The Mockito convention for throwing an exception from a void method is as follows:

```
doThrow(exception).when(mockObject).someVoidMethod();
```

We'll modify the test to stub the `process()` method in order to throw an exception. The following is the modified test code:

```
@Test
public void when_subsystem_throws_exception_Then_routes_to
  _error_page_() throws Exception {
  doThrow(new IllegalStateException("LDAP error")).
    when(loginController).process(request, response);
  when(request.getServletPath()).thenReturn("/logon.do");
```

```
    when(request.getRequestDispatcher(anyString()))
      .thenReturn(dispatcher);
    controller.doGet(request, response);
    verify(request).getRequestDispatcher(eq("error.jsp"));
    verify(dispatcher).forward(request, response);
}
```

When we run the test, it fails for an unhandled exception as exception handling has not been done yet. The following is the JUnit output:

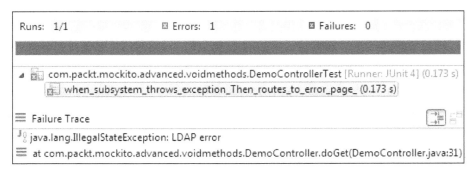

Modify the `DemoController` constructor to handle exceptions. The following is the modified code:

```
protected void doGet(HttpServletRequest req, HttpServletResponse
  res) throws ServletException, IOException {
  try {
    String urlContext = req.getServletPath();
    if (urlContext.equals("/")) {
      req.getRequestDispatcher("login.jsp").forward(req, res);
    } else if (urlContext.equals("/logon.do")) {
      loginController.process(req, res);
    } else {
      req.setAttribute("error", "Invalid request path '" +
        urlContext + "'");
      req.getRequestDispatcher("error.jsp").forward(req, res);
    }
  } catch (Exception ex) {
    req.setAttribute("error", ex.getMessage());
    req.getRequestDispatcher("error.jsp").forward(req, res);
  }

}
```

Rerunning the test passes execution; the following is the test output:

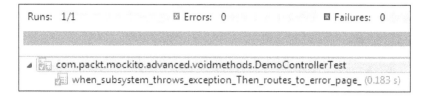

Working with void method callbacks

An external code dependency may process data in a void method, for example, it may send an e-mail or update a database row. We can easily stub a void method by mocking the dependency, but at times, void methods may change the input argument object's attribute, for example, it may set the error code of an `Error` object passed in as an argument, and we may use the modified value in our calculation. In this scenario, if we stub the void method, it doesn't help us to modify or add the stubbed method's argument attribute. As a result, our test might either fail or some portion of the code might remain untested.

Consider the exception handling code for `DemoController`. It retrieves the error message of the exception and passes the message to the end users, as the message might not be useful to the business users; it doesn't make any sense to us if we see a `NullPointerException` error while booking a movie ticket. Instead of passing the raw business exception to the user, the system should analyze the error message, form a useful error message, and pass a meaningful message to the end user.

We'll modify the `DemoController` code to analyze the `StackTrace` method, retrieve an error message code for the trace, look up the code for a meaningful error message, and pass the message to the user. We'll create an `Error` object with an array of `StackTraceElement` and an `errorCode` string. The following is the code:

```
public class Error {
  private StackTraceElement[] trace;
  private String errorCode;
  //Getters and setters are ignored for brevity
}
```

An `ErrorHandler` interface takes the `Error` object, maps the `StackTraceElements` method to an `errorCode` string, and sets the code back to the `Error` object. The following is the code body:

```
public interface ErrorHandler {

  void mapTo(Error error);
}
```

The `MessageRepository` interface looks up the error code and retrieves a meaningful message from the database. The following is the `MessageRepository` class:

```
public interface MessageRepository {
  String lookUp(String... errorCode);
}
```

The following modified `DemoController` code invokes the `ErrorHandler` and `MessageRepository` interface to get a meaningful message, and passes the message to the user.

```
} catch (Exception ex) {
  String errorMsg = ex.getMessage();
  Error errorDto = new Error();
  errorDto.setTrace(ex.getStackTrace());
  errorHandler.mapTo(errorDto);

  if(errorDto.getErrorCode() != null){
    errorMsg = messageRepository.lookUp (errorDto.
      getErrorCode());
  }
  req.setAttribute("error", errorMsg);
  req.getRequestDispatcher("error.jsp").forward(req, res);
}
```

We ignored the rest of the method and dependencies for brevity. You can download the code for details. The `mapTo` method takes an `Error` object and populates the `errorCode` string of the `Error` object. If no matching `errorCode` string is found, the `errorCode` remains as it is. If the `errorCode` string is found, the `errorCode` string is passed to `messageRepository` for an error message lookup.

When we mock the dependencies (`errorHandler` and `messageRepository`) and rerun the tests, some portion remains untested. The following is the screenshot of the untested code:

```java
        } catch (Exception ex) {

            String errorMsg = ex.getMessage();
            Error errorDto = new Error();
            errorHandler.mapTo(errorDto);

            if(errorDto.getErrorCode() != null){
                errorMsg = messageRepository.lookUp(errorDto.getErrorCode());
            }
            req.setAttribute("error", errorMsg);
            req.getRequestDispatcher("error.jsp").forward(req, res);
        }
```

We should modify the `Error` object from the `void mapTo` method to unit test the untested line. The `mapTo` method looks up the database to map a `StackTrace` method with an error code, so we must mock out the database call and stub the `void` method. The following are reasons behind mocking the database call, and you must configure your tests to adhere to these principles:

- **Fast execution**: Tests should be executed extremely fast, so that they can provide quick feedback. Would you care to wait for a build system that takes 2 hours to finish execution? This means if a test fails, you have to wait for 2 hours to verify your fix.
- **Tests should be reliable**: Tests should fail if the production code is broken. Your tests will be considered unreliable in the following situations:
  - You break the production logic, but the tests pass
  - You don't touch the production code, but your tests still fail
- **In-memory data dependent**: Tests should depend on in-memory data rather than pulling data from an external source, for instance, accessing the database for data can fail a test if the expected data is not present in the database for any reason, such as, if someone has deleted the data.

However, if we stub the `void` method, how can we set the `errorCode` string to the `Error` object? Also, we cannot directly set the `Error` object attributes as the object is created inside the catch block.

The resolution is Mockito's doAnswer() method. The doAnswer() method can intercept the void method call and access the void method arguments and the mock object. So, we can create our callback Answer implementation, access the Error object passed as an argument, and set an errorCode string to it. The following is the syntax for doAnswer():

```
doAnswer(answer).when(mock).someVoidMethod();
```

We'll create an anonymous Answer object , access the Error object, and set the errorCode string. The following is the code:

```
@Test
public void when_subsystem_throws_any_exception_Then_finds_
    error_message_and_routes_to_error_page_() throws Exception {
    doThrow(new IllegalStateException("LDAP error")).when
        (loginController).process(request, response);
    doAnswer(new Answer<Object>() {
      @Override
      public Object answer(InvocationOnMock invocation) throws
        Throwable {
        Error err = (Error)invocation.getArguments()[0];
        err.setErrorCode("123");
        return err;
      }
    }
    ).when(errorHandler).mapTo(isA(Error.class));

    when(request.getServletPath()).thenReturn("/logon.do");
    when(request.getRequestDispatcher(anyString()))
        .thenReturn(dispatcher);

    controller.doGet(request, response);

    verify(request).getRequestDispatcher(eq("error.jsp"));
    verify(dispatcher).forward(request, response);
}
```

The preceding change covers the untested lines. The following screenshot shows the test coverage output:

```
String errorMsg = ex.getMessage();
Error errorDto = new Error();
errorDto.setTrace(ex.getStackTrace());
errorHandler.mapTo(errorDto);

if(errorDto.getErrorCode() != null){
    errorMsg = messageRepository.lookUp(errorDto.getErrorCode());
}
req.setAttribute("error", errorMsg);
req.getRequestDispatcher("error.jsp").forward(req, res);
```

Learning doCallRealMethod and doNothing

In this section, we'll explore two methods, namely, doNothing and doCallRealMethod.

The doNothing() method does nothing. By default, when we create a mock object and call a void method on that mock object, the void method does not do anything, or rather, it is stubbed by default, but still, we stub void methods using doNothing() for void method chaining. If you need consecutive calls on a void method, the first call to throw an error, the next call to do nothing, and then the call after that to perform some logic using doAnswer(), then follow the ensuing syntax:

```
doThrow(new RuntimeException()).
doNothing().
doAnswer(someAnswer).
when(mock).someVoidMethod();
```

The doCallRealMethod() method is used when you want to call the real implementation of a method on a mock object. The following is the syntax:

```
doCallRealMethod().when(mock).someVoidMethod();
```

Exploring doReturn

The doReturn() method is like thenReturn(), but this is used only when when(mock).thenReturn(return) cannot be used. The when().thenReturn() method is more readable than doReturn(). Also, doReturn() is not type safe. The thenReturn method checks method return types and raises a compilation error if an unsafe type is passed. You can use doReturn() when working with spy objects. Here is the syntax for using the doReturn() test:

```
doReturn(value).when(mock).method(argument);
```

The following code snippet provides an example of unsafe usage of `doReturn`:

```
@Test
public void when_do_return_is_not_safe() throws Exception {
  when(request.getServletPath()).thenReturn("/logon.do");
  assertEquals("/logon.do", request.getServletPath());

  doReturn(1.111d).when(request.getServletPath());
  request.getServletPath();
}
```

The `request.getServletPath()` method returns a string value. If we try to stub the `request.getServletPath()` method with a double using `thenReturn`, the Java compiler will complain about the return type; but if we use `doReturn` and return a double value, the test fails at runtime. So `doReturn` has two drawbacks; it is unreadable and error prone. The following is the test output:

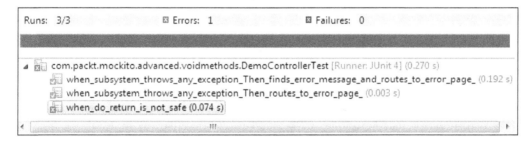

The following screenshot shows the failure trace:

```
Failure Trace
org.mockito.exceptions.misusing.UnfinishedStubbingException:
Unfinished stubbing detected here:
-> at com.packt.mockito.advanced.voidmethods.DemoControllerTest.
                    when_do_return_is_not_safe(DemoControllerTest.java:79)
E.g. thenReturn() may be missing.
Examples of correct stubbing:
    when(mock.isOk()).thenReturn(true);
    when(mock.isOk()).thenThrow(exception);
    doThrow(exception).when(mock).someVoidMethod();
```

The `doReturn` method becomes handy with spy objects. We'll explore `doReturn` in the spy section.

Verifying arguments using ArgumentCaptor

An `ArgumentCaptor` object verifies the arguments passed to a stubbed method. Sometimes, we create an object in our code under test and then pass it to a method on a mocked dependency, but never return it. Argument captors let us directly access these values provided to our mocks in order to examine them more closely. An **ArgumentCaptor** object provides an API to test the computed value.

In our exception handling code, we create an `Error` object, set exception trace to the object, invoke the `ErrorHandler` interface to map the `Error` object to an `errorCode` string, and finally, call the `MessageRepository` class to return a meaningful error message for the `errorCode` string. An `ArgumentCaptor` can return to us the argument details passed to a stubbed method.

Mockito verifies argument values in natural Java style by using the `equals()` method. This is also the recommended way for matching arguments because it makes tests clean and simple. In some situations though, it is helpful to assert on certain arguments after the actual verification.

An `ArgumentCaptor` object is defined as follows:

```
ArgumentCaptor<T> argCaptor= ArgumentCaptor.forClass(T.class);
```

Where `T` is the type of argument, such as a string or a user-defined class.

The following syntax is used to capture arguments:

```
verify(mockObject).methodA(argCaptor.capture());
```

If an `ArgumentCaptor` object captures arguments for multiple invocations, the captured values can be retrieved by calling the `getAllValues()` method. The `getAllValues()` method returns `List<T>` and the `getValue()` method returns `T`, which is the last method invocation result. Here, `T` is the type of argument class, such as an integer or any Java class type.

The following code uses an `ArgumentCaptor` to verify the argument passed into the `lookUp` method.

```
ArgumentCaptor<String> captor = ArgumentCaptor.forClass
    (String.class);
verify(repository).lookUp(captor.capture());
assertEquals("123", captor.getValue());
```

Working with generic collection arguments

The following example demonstrates how to capture collection arguments. Create an interface and add a method to accept a list of strings. The following is the code:

```
interface Service{
  void call(List<String> args);
}
```

Try to create an `ArgumentCapture` for the list of strings. You cannot create a class for `List<String>.class`, so you can try to use `List.class`. The following screenshot shows you the Java compilation error while converting `List.class` to `List<String>`:

```
@Test
public void when_captures_collections() throws Exception {
    ArgumentCaptor<List<String>> captor
    = ArgumentCaptor.forClass(List.class);
}
```
 Type mismatch: cannot convert from ArgumentCaptor<List> to ArgumentCaptor<List<String>>
interf 1 quick fix available:
   vo   Change type of 'captor' to 'ArgumentCaptor<List>'
}   Press 'F2' for focus

The following code snippet creates `List.class` and casts it to `Class<List<String>>`, and passes it to `ArgumentCaptor`. This will give you warnings about unsafe casts; you can suppress the warning by annotating the construct with `@SuppressWarnings("unchecked")`:

```
@Test
public void when_captures_collections() throws Exception {
  Class<List<String>> listClass = (Class<List<String>>)
    (Class)List.class;
  ArgumentCaptor<List<String>> captor = ArgumentCaptor.forClass
    (listClass);
}
```

The following test provides an example of such a use. Here, `service` is a mocked implementation of the `Service` interface:

```
@Test public void when_captures_collections(){
  Class<List<String>> listClass = (Class<List<String>>)(Class)
    List.class;
  ArgumentCaptor<List<String>> captor = ArgumentCaptor.forClass
    (listClass);
```

```
    service.call(Arrays.asList("a","b"));
    verify(service).call(captor.capture());
    assertTrue(captor.getValue().
    containsAll(Arrays.asList("a","b")));
}
```

Working with variable arguments and arrays

The following example shows you how to capture an argument of type arrays or var-args (T... t).

Modify the MessageRepository class to accept variable arguments of strings as errorCodes. The following is the modified code:

```
public interface MessageRepository {
    String lookUp(String... errorCode);
}
```

Create a test to pass an array to the lookUp method and capture values. The following is the code snippet:

```
@Test
public void when_capturing_variable_args() throws Exception {
    String[] errorCodes = {"a","b","c"};

    ArgumentCaptor<String> captor = ArgumentCaptor.forClass
        (String.class);
    repository.lookUp(errorCodes);
    verify(repository).lookUp(captor.capture(),captor.capture()
        ,captor.capture());
    assertTrue(captor.getAllValues().containsAll(Arrays.asList
        (errorCodes)));
}
```

The following Mockito URL has the fix for the variable argument capture:

https://github.com/mockito/mockito/commit/
e43a958833df5aa46f54d7cd83b1c17fa19cc5dc

ArgumentCaptor is modified in a default branch to capture variable arguments. The following is the code snippet:

```
    verify(messageRepository).lookUp(argumentCaptor.captureVararg());
```

[Note that this fix is not available in the latest Mockito build 1.9.5.]

Verifying an invocation order

Mockito facilitates verification if interactions with a mock were performed in a given order using the `InOrder` API. It allows us to create an `InOrder` of mocks and verify the call order of all the calls of all the mocks.

`InOrder` is created with mock object using the following syntax:

```
InOrder inOrder=inOrder(mock1,mock2,...mockN);
```

Method invocation order is checked using the following syntax:

```
inOrder.verify(mock1).methodCall1();
inOrder.verify(mock2).methodCall2();
```

If `methodCall2()` of `mock2` is invoked before `methodCall1()` of `mock1`, the test fails. The following test verifies the test order:

```
@Test
public void when_inorder() throws Exception {
  request.getServletPath();
  service.call(Arrays.asList("a","b"));
  InOrder inOrder=inOrder(request,service);
  inOrder.verify(service).call(anyList());
  inOrder.verify(request).getServletPath();
}
```

The test verifies that the `call()` method is invoked before the `getServletPath()` method, but the methods were invoked in reverse order, so the test will fail. The following screenshot demonstrates the error:

```
≡ Failure Trace                                                    ⊟ ⊟

J org.mockito.exceptions.verification.VerificationInOrderFailure:
  Verification in order failure
  Wanted but not invoked:
  request.getServletPath();
≡ -> at com.packt.mockito.advanced.voidmethods.DemoControllerTest.when_inorder
```

Reordering the verification sequence in the following manner fixes the test:

```
@Test public void when_inorder() throws Exception {
    request.getServletPath();
    service.call(Arrays.asList("a","b"));
    InOrder inOrder=inOrder(request,service);
    inOrder.verify(request).getServletPath();
    inOrder.verify(service).call(anyList());
}
```

Spying objects

A Mockito spy allows us to use real objects instead of mocks by replacing some of the methods with stubbed ones. This behavior allows us to test the legacy code. The spy is useful for legacy code as you cannot invoke a few testing impediment methods from your code under test, and also, you cannot mock a class that needs to be tested. A spy can stub these testing impediments without mocking the code under test. A spy can stub the nontestable methods so that other methods can be tested easily. You can also use spies without doing any stubbing and just use them to verify interactions between two totally real objects.

Once an expectation is set for a method on a `spy` object, the `spy` object no longer returns the original value. It starts returning the stubbed value, but still exhibits the original behavior for the other methods that are not stubbed.

Mockito can create a spy for a real object. Unlike stubbing, when we use the spy object, real methods are called (unless a method was stubbed).

Spy is also known as partial mock. The following is the declaration of `spy`:

```
SomeClass realObject = new RealImplemenation();
SomeClass spyObject = spy(realObject);
```

The following is a self-explanatory example of `spy`:

```
@Test
public void when_spying_real_objects() throws Exception {
    Error error = new Error();
    error.setErrorCode("Q123");
    Error spyError = spy(error);
    //call real method from  spy
    assertEquals("Q123", spyError.getErrorCode());

    //Changing value using spy
    spyError.setErrorCode(null);

    //verify spy has the changed value
```

```
        assertEquals(null, spyError.getErrorCode());

        //Stubbing method
        when(spyError.getErrorCode()).thenReturn("E456");

        //Changing value using spy
        spyError.setErrorCode(null);

        //Stubbed method value E456 is returned NOT NULL
        assertNotEquals(null, spyError.getErrorCode());

        //Stubbed method value E456
        assertEquals("E456", spyError.getErrorCode());
    }
```

Spying real objects and calling real methods on a spy object has side effects; to immunize this side effect, use doReturn() instead of thenReturn().

The following code describes the side effect of spying and calling thenReturn():

```
@Test
public void when_doReturn_fails() throws Exception {
    List<String> list = new ArrayList<String>();
    List<String> spy = spy(list);
    //impossible the real list.get(0) is called and fails
    //with IndexOutofBoundsException, as the list is empty
    when(spy.get(0)).thenReturn("not reachable");
}
```

The spy object calls a real method when trying to stub get(index), and unlike the mock objects, the real method was called and it failed with an ArrayIndexOutOfBounds error. The following screenshot displays the failure message:

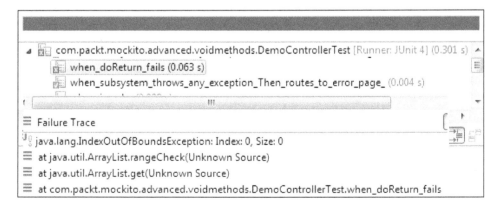

This failure can be protected using `doReturn()`, as shown is the following code:

```
@Test public void when_doReturn_fails() throws Exception {
  List<String> list = new ArrayList<String>();
  List<String> spy = spy(list);

  //doReturn fixed the issue
  doReturn("now reachable").when(spy).get(0);
  assertEquals("now reachable", spy.get(0));
}
```

Exploring Mockito annotations

We learned that Mockito supports the `@Mock` annotation for mocking. Like `@Mock`, Mockito offers three useful annotations, namely, `@Spy`, `@Captor`, and `@InjectMocks`:

- `@Captor`: This simplifies the creation of `ArgumentCaptor`, and this is useful when the argument to capture is a horrible generic class
- `@Spy`: This creates the spy of a given object; use it instead of `spy(Object)`
- `@InjectMocks`: It injects mock or spy fields into tested objects automatically using **constructor** injection, **setter** injection, or **field** injection

The following example demonstrates the `@captor` annotation:

```
@RunWith(MockitoJUnitRunner.class)
public class AnnotationTest {

  @Captor
  ArgumentCaptor<List<String>> captor;
  @Mock Service service;

  @Test
  public void when_captor_annotation_is_used() {
    service.call(Arrays.asList("a","b"));
    verify(service).call(captor.capture());
    assertTrue(captor.getValue().containsAll(Arrays.
      asList("a","b")));
  }
}
```

The annotation creates the `ArgumentCaptor` object, and we don't need to typecast it to `Class<List<String>>`.

The following example demonstrates the use of the `@spy` annotation:

```
@RunWith(MockitoJUnitRunner.class)
public class SpyAnnotationTest {

  @Spy
  ErrorHandlerImpl errorHandler;

  @Test
  public void when_spy_annotation_is_used() throws Exception {
    assertNotNull(errorHandler);
  }
}
```

A `Spy` object of `ErrorHandlerImpl` is created automatically for `errorHandler`. You cannot create a spy for an interface. The following error message pops up when we try to create a spy for the `ErrorHandler` interface:

```
@Spy
ErrorHandler errorHandler;
```

The following screenshot displays the error message:

≡ Failure Trace
org.mockito.exceptions.base.MockitoException:
Cannot instantiate a @Spy for 'errorHandler' field.
≡ You haven't provided the instance for spying at field declaration so I tried to construct the instance.
However, I failed because: the type 'ErrorHandler' is an interface.
Examples of correct usage of @Spy:
    @Spy List mock = new LinkedList();
    @Spy Foo foo; //only if Foo has parameterless constructor
    //also, don't forget about MockitoAnnotations.initMocks();

The following example demonstrates the use of the `@InjectMocks` annotation. Here, we'll create a `@spy` annotation and two `@mocks` annotations. The `@InjectMocks` annotation sets the mocks and spy to the real object as a constructor injection.

```
@RunWith(MockitoJUnitRunner.class)
public class InjectMocksAnnotationTest {

  @Mock LoginController loginController;
  @Mock MessageRepository repository;
  @Spy ErrorHandlerImpl errorHandler;

  @InjectMocks
```

```
DemoController controller;

@Mock HttpServletRequest request;
@Mock HttpServletResponse response;
@Mock RequestDispatcher dispatcher;

@Test
public void when_mocks_are_injected() throws Exception {
  when(request.getServletPath()).thenReturn("/");
  when(request.getRequestDispatcher(anyString())).thenReturn
    (dispatcher);
  controller.doGet(request, response);
  verify(request).getRequestDispatcher(eq("login.jsp"));
}
}
```

The DemoController constructor depends on three classes; the preceding example creates the mock and spy objects and injects them to the DemoController constructor.

Changing the default Mockito settings

We learned that nonstubbed methods of a mock object return default values, such as Null for an object and false for a Boolean. However, Mockito allows us to change the default settings to return other nondefault values; these are basically preconfigured answers. The following are settings that are allowed:

- RETURNS_DEFAULTS: This is the default setting that returns null for an object, false for a Boolean, and so on.

- RETURNS_SMART_NULLS: This returns *smart nulls*, which are stubs that act like nulls (in that they throw exceptions if you try and call stub. anyMethod()), but throw exceptions that are much more useful than normal NullPointerExceptions by giving you information on which call they came from and where.

- RETURNS_MOCKS: This returns mock for objects and default value for primitives. If the object cannot be mocked (such as a final class), a Null value is returned.

- RETURNS_DEEP_STUBS: This returns a deep stub. This is really important for legacy code where we need to stub the method chaining, for example, when Foo calls getBar().getTar().getName(). Deep stubbing allows Foo to directly stub the getName() method to return a value. Otherwise, we have to stub Foo's getBar method to return a mock Bar object, stub the bar's getTar() method to return a mock Tar object, and finally, stub the Tar's getName method to return a value.

- CALLS_REAL_METHODS: This calls the corresponding method from the real implementation of the mocked class.

The following example overrides the default Mockito settings and uses different return types. Suppose we have the following classes:

```
class Foo {
  Bar bar;
  //Getter and setter
}
class Bar {
  Tar tar;
  //Getter and setter
}
class Tar {
  private String name;
  //Getter and setter
}
```

The following test case uses the RETURNS_DEFAULTS setting to return a NULL Bar object:

```
@Test
public void when_default_settings() throws Exception {

  Foo fooWithReturnDefault = Mockito.mock(Foo.class,
    Mockito.RETURNS_DEFAULTS);
  // default null is returned
  assertNull(fooWithReturnDefault.getBar());
}
```

The following test case uses the RETURNS_SMART_NULLS setting to return a smart NULL object:

```
@Test
public void when_changing_default_settings_to_return_smartNULLS(){

  Foo fooWithSmartNull = Mockito.mock(Foo.class, Mockito.RETURNS_
    SMART_NULLS);
```

```
    // a smart null is returned
    assertNotNull(fooWithSmartNull.getBar());
    System.out.println("fooWithSmartNull.getBar() =" + fooWith
      SmartNull.getBar());
}
```

The following is the System.out output:

```
fooWithSmartNull.getBar() =SmartNull returned by this unstubbed method
call on a mock:foo.getBar();
```

The following test case uses the RETURNS_MOCKS setting to return a mock object hierarchy:

```
@Test
public void when_changing_default_settings_to_return_mocks() {

    Foo fooWithReturnsMocks = Mockito.mock(Foo.class, Mockito.
      RETURNS_MOCKS);
    // a mock is returned
    Bar mockBar = fooWithReturnsMocks.getBar();
    assertNotNull(mockBar);
    assertNotNull(mockBar.getTar());
    assertNotNull(mockBar.getTar().getName());
    System.out.println("fooWithReturnsMocks.getBar()=" + mockBar);
    System.out.println("fooWithReturnsMocks.getBar().getTar().
      getName()={" + mockBar.getTar().getName()+"}");
}
```

The RETURNS_MOCKS setting populates the Foo object with a mocked Bar object. A mocked Bar object has a mocked Tar object and the mocked Tar object has an empty mocked string name. The following is the output:

```
fooWithReturnsMocks.getBar()=Mock for Bar, hashCode: 1620275837
fooWithReturnsMocks.getBar().getTar().getName()={}
```

The following test case uses the RETURNS_DEEP_STUBS setting to return a deep-stubbed object hierarchy:

```
@Test
public void when_returns_deep_stub() throws Exception {
    Foo fooWithDeepStub = Mockito.mock(Foo.class, Mockito.
      RETURNS_DEEP_STUBS);
    when(fooWithDeepStub.getBar().getTar().getName()).
      thenReturn("Deep Stub");
    // a deep stubbed mock is returned
```

```
    System.out.println("fooWithDeepStub.getBar().getTar().
      getName()="+ fooWithDeepStub.getBar().getTar().getName());
    assertNotNull(fooWithDeepStub.getBar().getTar().getName());
  }
```

The RETURNS_DEEP_STUBS setting is very useful for legacy code. In the preceding example, we had to stub the getName() method of a Tar object, but to stub the method, we had to mock a series of other objects. Only when we used the RETURNS_DEEP_STUBS setting could the chaining of the method call stub the method and other objects.

The following is the print output:

```
fooWithDeepStub.getBar().getTar().getName()=Deep Stub
```

Resetting mock objects

A static method reset(T...) enables the resetting of mock objects. The reset() method clears the stubs.

The following code snippet stubs the getName() method of a mocked Bar object. After resetting the getName() method, the stubbing gets cleared and starts returning the default NULL value.

```
@Test
public void when_resetting_mocks() throws Exception {
  Bar bar= Mockito.mock(Bar.class);
  when(bar.getName()).thenReturn("***");
  assertNotNull(bar.getName());
  reset(bar);
  //Bar is reset, the getName() stub is cleared
  assertNull(bar.getName());
}
```

Resetting mocks is not recommended as it's a sign that your test is probably doing too much, and you should probably just have another test with fresh mocks instead.

Working with inline stubbing

Mockito allows us to create mocks while stubbing it. Basically, it allows you to create a stub in one line of code. This can be helpful to keep the test code clean. For example, some stubs can be created and stubbed during field initialization in a test:

```
public class InlineStubbing {

  Bar bar =  when(mock(Bar.class).getTar()).thenReturn(new
    Tar()).getMock();
```

```
@Test
public void when_stubbing_inline() throws Exception {
  assertNotNull(bar);
  assertNotNull(bar.getTar());
}

}
```

The bar object is stubbed and created at the same time. This is useful when the bar object is used in many test cases within the test class. The bar object should always return a Tar object.

Determining mock details

Sometimes, we need to determine whether an object is a mock or a spy. This situation can arise when an object uses the @injectMocks annotation; it can inject a spy or a mock object. We can find out the type using Mockito.mockingDetails. It can identify whether a particular object is a mock or a spy.

The following example demonstrates the Mockito.mockingDetails API.

The ServiceImpl class has two dependencies, namely, Dependency1 and Dependency2.

```
class Dependency1{

}
class Dependency2{

}
```

The following is the ServiceImpl class:

```
class ServiceImpl{
  private final Dependency1 dependency1;
  private final Dependency2 dependency2;
  public ServiceImpl(Dependency1 dependency1, Dependency2
    dependency2) {
    this.dependency1 = dependency1;
    this.dependency2 = dependency2;
  }
  public Dependency1 getDependency1() {
    return dependency1;
  }
  public Dependency2 getDependency2() {
    return dependency2;
  }

}
```

The following test demonstrates the usage of mockingDetails:

```
import static org.mockito.Mockito.mockingDetails;

@RunWith(MockitoJUnitRunner.class)
public class MockDetailsTest {
    @Spy Dependency1 dep;
    @Mock Dependency1 dep1;
    @Mock Dependency2 dep2;
    @InjectMocks  ServiceImpl service;

    @Test public void when_determining_type() throws Exception {
        assertNotNull(service);
        assertTrue(mockingDetails(service.getDependency2()).isMock());
        assertTrue(mockingDetails(dep).isSpy());
    }
}
```

The Service object can be populated with a stub or a mock Dependency1. We verified that Dependency2 is a mock and dep1 is a spy. We can also verify service.getDependency1() to check whether a mock or a stub was injected.

Summary

This chapter covered the advanced Mockito framework topics such as working with void methods, throwing exception from void methods, writing callbacks for void methods, returning value using doReturn, void method chaining, and calling original method. It also covered Mockito annotations, verifying arguments using argument captor, verifying an invocation order, spying objects using spy, changing default Mockito settings, resetting mock objects, inline stubbing, and mock details.

By now, you should be able to use advanced Mockito features.

The next chapter in line, *Behavior-driven Development with Mockito*, covers the BDD concepts, scenarios, test conventions, and examples of BDD with Mockito.

4
Behavior-driven Development with Mockito

"Computer science is no more about computers than astronomy is about telescopes."

– Edsger Dijkstra

This chapter explores **Behavior-driven Development (BDD)** and how BDD can help you minimize project failure risks. The following topics are covered in this chapter:

- Understanding the context of BDD
- Exploring BDD
- Exercising BDD with Mockito

Understanding the context of BDD

This section deals with the software development strategies, drawbacks, and conquering the shortcomings of traditional approaches. The following strategies are applied to deliver software products to customers:

- Top-down or waterfall approach
- Bottom-up approach

We'll cover these two approaches in the following sections.

The following key people/roles/stakeholders are involved in software development:

- **Customers**: They explore the concept and identify the high-level goal of the system, such as automating the expense claim process
- **Analysts**: They analyze the requirements, work with the customer to understand the system, and build the system requirement specifications
- **Designers/architects**: They visualize the system, design the baseline architecture, identify the components, interact and handle the nonfunctional requirements, such as scalability and availability
- **Developers**: They construct the system from the design and specification documents
- **Testers**: They design test cases and verify the implementation
- **Operational folks**: They install the software as per the customer's environment
- **Maintenance team**: They handle bugs and monitor the system's health
- **Managers**: They act as facilitators and keep track of the progress and schedule

Exploring the top-down strategy

In the top-down strategy, analysts analyze the requirements and hand over the use cases / functional specifications to the designers and architects for designing the system. The architects/designers design the baseline architecture, identify the system components and interactions, and then pass the design over to the developers for implementation. The testers then verify the implementation (might report bugs for fixing), and finally, the software is deployed to the customer's environment.

The following diagram depicts the top-down flow from requirement engineering to maintenance:

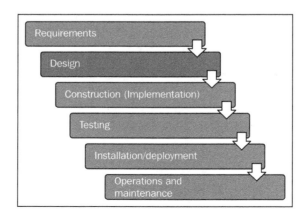

The biggest drawback of this approach is the cost of rework. For instance, if the development team finds that a requirement is not feasible, they consult the design or analysis team. Then the architects or analysts look at the issue and rework the analysis or design. This approach has a cascading effect; the cost of rework is very high. Customers rarely know what they want before they see the system in action. Building everything all at once is a quick way to cause your requirements to change. Even without the difference in cost of requirement changes, you'll have fewer changes if you write the requirements later in the process, when you have a partially working product that the customer can see and everybody has more information about how the product will work.

Exploring the bottom-up strategy

In the bottom-up strategy, the requirement is broken into small chunks and each chunk is designed, developed, and unit tested separately, and finally, the chunks are integrated. The individual base elements of the system are first specified in great detail. These elements are then linked together to form larger subsystems, which in turn are linked until a complete top-level system is formed. Each subsystem is developed in isolation from the other subsystems, so integration is very important in the bottom-up approach. If integration fails, the cost and effort of building the subsystems gets jeopardized. Suppose you are building a healthcare system with three subsystems, namely, patient management, receivable management, and the claims module. If the patient module cannot talk to the claims module, the system fails. The effort of building the patient management and claims management subsystems is just wasted. Agile development methodology would suggest building the functionality feature by feature across subsystems, that is, building a very basic patient management and claims management subsystem to make the functionality work initially, and then adding more to both simultaneously, to support each new feature that is required.

Finding the gaps

In real-life projects, the following is the percentage of feature usage:

- 60 percent of features are never used
- 30 percent of features are occasionally used
- 10 percent of features are frequently used

However, in the top-down approach, the analyst pays attention and brainstorms to create system requirements for all the features. In the top-down approach, time is spent to build a system where 90 percent of features are either not used or occasionally used. Instead, we can identify the high-value features and start building the features instead of paying attention to the low priority features, by using the bottom-up approach.

In the bottom-up approach, subsystems are built in isolation from each other, and this causes integration problems. If we prioritize the requirements and start with the highest priority feature, design the feature, build it, unit test it, integrate it, and then show a demo to the stakeholders (customers, analysts, product managers, and so on), we can easily identify the gaps and reduce the risk of rework. We can then pick the next feature and follow the steps (designing, coding, testing, and getting feedback from the customers), and finally integrate the feature with the existing system. This reduces the integration issues of the bottom-up approach.

The following figure represents the approach. Each feature is analyzed, designed, coded, tested, and integrated separately. An example of a requirement could be *login failure error messages appear red and in bold*, while a feature could be *incorrect logins are rejected*. Typically, it should be a little larger and a useful standalone bit of functionality, rather than a specific single requirement for that functionality.

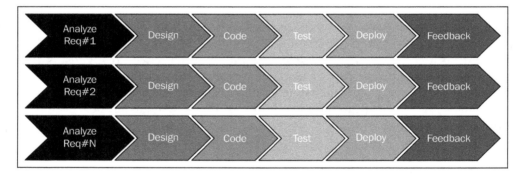

Another problem associated with software development is communication; each stakeholder has a different vocabulary and this causes issues for common understanding.

The following are the best practices to minimize software delivery risks:

- Focus on high-value, frequently used features.
- Build a common vocabulary for the stakeholders; a domain-specific language that anybody can understand.

- No more big-fat upfront designing. Evolve the design with the requirements, iteratively.

- Code to satisfy the current requirement. Don't code for a future requirement, which may or may not be delivered. Follow the **YAGNI (You Aren't Going to Need It)** principle.

- Build test the safety net for each requirement.

- Integrate the code with the system and rerun the regression test.

- Get feedback from the stakeholders and make immediate changes.

BDD suggests the preceding best approaches. The following section talks about BDD.

Exploring BDD

BDD is a software engineering process based on **Test-driven Development (TDD)**. Martin Fowler explains TDD on the following URL:

```
http://martinfowler.com/bliki/TestDrivenDevelopment.html
```

BDD combines the best practices of TDD, **Domain-driven Development (DDD)**, and **Object Oriented Programming (OOPs)**. You can learn about DDD on the following URL:

```
http://martinfowler.com/tags/domain%20driven%20design.html
```

In an agile team, scoping a feature is a mammoth task; the business stakeholders talk about business interests and the development team talks about technical challenges. BDD provides a universal language that allows useful communication and feedback between the stakeholders.

Agile methodologies include Scrum, Lean, Kanban, XP, and so on. Agile methodologies believe in self-organized teams. You can get more information about agile development on the following URL:

```
http://www.versionone.com/Agile101/Agile-Development-Methodologies-Scrum-Kanban-Lean-XP/
```

Dan North developed BDD and created the JBehave framework for BDD. He defines BDD as follows:

"Behavior-driven Development is about implementing an application by describing it from the point of view of its stakeholders."

He proposed the following best practices:

- Unit test names should start with the word *should* and should be written in order of business value.

- Acceptance tests are different from unit tests; unit tests are written by the developers whereas acceptance tests are written by analysts and other stakeholders. Acceptance testing is carried out to assess the system's acceptance against the business rules. **Acceptance tests (AT)** should be written in a user story manner, for example, **As a** *[role]* **I want** *[feature]* **so that** *[benefit]*. You can get more information about acceptance tests at the following URL:

  ```
  http://c2.com/cgi/wiki?AcceptanceTest
  ```

- Acceptance criteria should be written in terms of scenarios and implemented in the following manner:

  Given *[initial context]*, **when** *[event occurs]*, **then** *[ensure some outcomes]*

A user story describes a testable requirement, and a scenario defines the completeness or acceptance criteria of a story.

Let us write a user story for our stock broker simulation:

- **Story**: A stock is sold **in order to** maximize the profit. **As a** *stock broker*, **I want to** *sell a stock* **when** *the price goes up by 10 percent*.

The following is a scenario example:

- **Scenario**: 10 percent increase in stock price should sell the stock to the market. **Given** *a customer previously bought 'FB' stocks at $10.00/per* **share and** *he currently has 10 shares left in his portfolio* **when** *the 'FB' stock price becomes $11.00*, **then** *I should sell all the 'FB' stocks and the portfolio should have zero 'FB' stocks*.

Mockito supports the BDD style of writing tests, using the **given-when-then** syntax.

Exercising BDD with Mockito

In BDD, *given* represents the initial context and *when* represents the event/condition, but Mockito already has a *when* style (initial context definition) of method stubbing. Therefore, *when* doesn't go well with BDD. Thus, the BDDMockito class introduces an alias, so that we can stub method calls with the given(Object) method.

The following JUnit test is implemented in the BDD style:

```
@RunWith(MockitoJUnitRunner.class)
public class StockBrokerBDDTest {
  @Mock MarketWatcher marketWatcher;
  @Mock Portfolio portfolio;

  StockBroker broker;

  @Before public void setUp() {
    broker = new StockBroker(marketWatcher);
  }

  @Test
  public void should_sell_a_stock_when_price_increases_
    by_ten_percent(){
    Stock aCorp = new Stock("FB", "FaceBook", new BigDecimal
      (11.20));
    //Given a customer previously bought 10 'FB' stocks at
      //$10.00/per share
    given(portfolio.getAvgPrice(isA(Stock.class))).willReturn(new
      BigDecimal("10.00"));

    given(marketWatcher.getQuote(eq("FB"))).willReturn(aCorp);

    //when the 'FB' stock price becomes $11.00
    broker.perform(portfolio, aCorp);

    //then the 'FB' stocks are sold
    verify(portfolio).sell(aCorp,10);
  }
}
```

Note, the test name starts with a `should` statement. Mockito's given syntax is used to set the initial context that the portfolio already has 'FB' stocks bought at $10.00/ share and the current FB stock price is $11.00.

The following is the test execution output:

The BDD syntax

The following methods are used in conjunction with the `given` condition:

- `willReturn` (a value to be returned): This method returns a given value
- `willThrow` (a throwable to be thrown): This method throws a given exception
- `will` (`Answer` answer) and `willAnswer` (`Answer` answer): These methods are similar to `then(answer)` and `thenAnswer(answer)`
- `willCallRealMethod()`: This method calls the real method on the mock object/spy

> **jMock** and **EasyMock** are the two other Java-based unit testing frameworks that support mocking for automated unit tests.
>
> To learn about BDD and JBehave, visit the following URLs:
> - `http://jbehave.org/`
> - `http://www.infoq.com/presentations/bdd-dan-north/`

Summary

This chapter covered BDD concepts, BDD examples, and how we can write BDD-style tests with Mockito.

Now, you will be able to practice BDD and write BDD-style unit tests with Mockito.

The next chapter, *Unit Testing the Legacy Code with Mockito*, will cover the legacy code, testing impediments, design for testability, and unit testing the legacy code with Mockito.

5

Unit Testing the Legacy Code with Mockito

"Legacy code. The phrase strikes disgust in the hearts of programmers. It conjures images of slogging through a murky swamp of tangled undergrowth with leaches beneath and stinging flies above. It conjures odors of murk, slime, stagnancy, and offal. Although our first joy of programming may have been intense, the misery of dealing with legacy code is often sufficient to extinguish that flame."

– Michael C. Feathers, Working Effectively with Legacy Code

This chapter explores the following topics:

- Understanding the legacy code
- Working with testing impediments
- Exploring PowerMock
- Designing for testability with Mockito and PowerMock

Understanding the legacy code

The term **legacy** is frequently used as a slang to describe a complex code, which is difficult to understand, rigid, fragile in nature, and almost impossible to enhance.

But Michael Feathers, author of the legacy code refactoring book *Working Effectively with Legacy Code*, defines that any code with no automated unit tests is a legacy code. A piece of code could be well written, follow coding guidelines, easy to understand, clean, loosely coupled, and very easy to extend, but if it doesn't have automated unit tests, it is a legacy code.

Usually, fixing bugs or adding new features to a legacy project is very difficult compared to doing the same to a greenfield project. In legacy code, either automated unit tests do not exist or very few tests are written; the code is not designed for testability.

Winston Churchill said, "*We make a living by what we get, but we make a life by what we give.*"

We inherit legacy code from someone else, it could come from a very old project, from another team that cannot maintain the code, or it could be acquired from another company; but it is our duty to improve the quality.

Unit tests give us some level of assurance that our code is doing what the code is expected to do and allow us to change the code quickly and verify the change faster.

In general, legacy code is not testable and requires code structure change (refactoring) to make it testable, but the dilemma is, most of the time, the legacy system is so crucial to the business that no one dares to touch the code. It makes no sense to modify an existing crucial module unless something is seriously wrong. Stalemate! You cannot refactor code unless you have the automated test suite, because without tests, you have no idea whether you've changed or broken the system, and you cannot write tests, as the code needs refactoring.

Sometimes, it feels like legacy code, even with unit tests, is hard to understand, maintain, and enhance. We need to be careful to make our tests especially readable and to avoid close coupling with the actual implementation details.

To learn more about legacy code, you can read the legacy code Bible — *Working Effectively with Legacy code, Michael Feathers*. The following is the URL to the book:

```
http://www.amazon.com/Working-Effectively-Legacy-Michael-Feathers/
dp/0131177052
```

Exploring testing impediments

This section explains the nature or quality of code that makes unit testing difficult. Automated tests help us develop software quickly, even when we have a large code base to work on. Automated unit tests should be executed very fast so that the tests can give us quick feedback, however we cannot unit test code when it exhibits any of the following symptoms:

- Performs long running operations
- Connects to a database and modifies database records
- Performs remote computing — RMI

- Looks up JNDI resources or web/application server objects
- Accesses filesystems
- Works with native objects or graphical widgets (UI components, Windows alerts, JAVA Swing components, and so on)
- Accesses network resources (LAN printer, downloads data from the Internet, and so on)

Unit tests should not wait for a long running process to complete; it will defeat the purpose of quick feedback.

Unit tests should be reliable and they should fail if, and only if, the production code breaks. However, if your unit test verifies an I/O operation, such as connecting to a LAN printer, which is slow, error prone, and unpredictable, your unit test may fail for some network issue, but it will incorrectly signal that the code is broken. So unit testing a network operation defeats the test reliability principle. If you depend on anything in your unit tests that's unreliable (such as LAN connections, databases, random numbers, and so on), in turn, you make your tests unreliable. Testing is about getting confidence that your code is correct, and unreliability destroys confidence.

Unit tests run automatically, so it doesn't make any sense to open a modal dialog or show an alert message during test execution, because the test will wait, unless the UI dialog or the alert is closed.

Working with PowerMock

Sometimes, we cannot unit test our code, as the special Java constructs hide the testing impediments (a LAN connection or database connection in a private method, final method, static method, or initialization block), such as private methods, final methods and classes, static methods and initialization blocks, new operator, and so on. We refactor code for testability (explained in the *Designing for testability with Mockito* section) and, sometimes, compromise a good design for the sole purpose of testability. For example, final classes and methods are avoided, private methods are converted to protected or default, or unnecessarily moved to a collaborator class, static methods are avoided completely, and so on. This is done simply because of the limitations of the existing frameworks. Also, these aren't just feature limitations; they are intentional choices. Mockito could do the things PowerMock does, but it doesn't because those are test smells and strong indications that you are following a poor design. Many of these are bad designs by themselves even outside testability and/or things you shouldn't do even in the name of testability. For example, the static method involves direct coupling between random chunks of code, directly subverting good OO design and encapsulation.

Converting private methods to protected ones so that you can stub internal methods is not a good testing design. Partial mocks are typically code smell against the SRP, and refactoring such things into another class makes for a better design!

Code with final methods typically protects a specific implementation, and that should imply that such implementations have an interface that can be stubbed instead.

Some design decisions taken without the pressure of the testability result with little thought for it (static/final/no SRP), and this results in code that is actively difficult to test. These are not things people should be doing intentionally, and then use PowerMock as a matter of recourse. PowerMock is a fallback for legacy code that they should aim to stop using with time.

PowerMock provides special mocking capabilities and allows us to unit test code even when the special Java constructs hide the testing impediments. PowerMock is a framework that extends other mock libraries, such as EasyMock and Mockito, with more powerful capabilities. PowerMock uses a custom classloader and bytecode manipulation to enable mocking of static methods, constructors, final classes and methods, private methods, removal of static initializers, and so on. PowerMock is essential for legacy code.

The following is the website for PowerMock:

`www.powermock.org`

PowerMock's distribution for EasyMock and Mockito can be downloaded from the following website:

`URL:https://code.google.com/p/powermock/wiki/Downloads?tm=2`

Download the `powermock-mockito-junit-1.5.5.zip` file for Mockito and JUnit. The ZIP file contains the `powermock-mockito-1.5.5-full.jar` file and its dependencies.

The following examples explore the Mockito extension API, also known as `PowerMockito`.

You need to annotate the test class with the `@RunWith(PowerMockRunner.class)` annotation in order to bootstrap PowerMock. The classes that cannot be mocked need to be prepared for testability by using the `@PrepareForTest` annotation.

We'll create a Java project to unit test the PowerMockito capabilities. The following are the steps to set up the project:

1. Create a Java project named `UnitTestingLegacyCode`.

2. Extract the `powermock-mockito-junit-1.5.5.zip` file, copy the JAR files, and add to the project's classpath.

3. Create two source folders, namely, `src` and `test`, and add the `com.packt.legacy.powermockito` packages to them. The following figure displays the project structure:

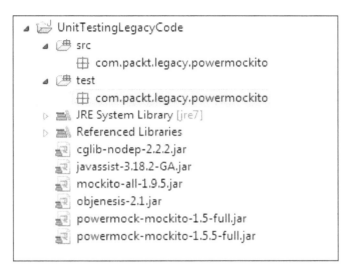

We'll examine the mocking capabilities of PowerMockito for untestable constructs, such as private method, static method, initialization blocks, final classes and methods, and constructor and super constructor.

 You can get more information from the following URL:
`https://code.google.com/p/powermock/wiki/SuppressUnwantedBehavior`

Stubbing static methods

This section deals with static methods. You cannot stub a static method with Mockito, but PowerMockito allows us to stub static methods. The following `MedicalBill` class generates the medical bill ID; the `generateId()` method is a static method and, in real life, it calls the database to generate an identifier. For simplicity, we will call the random number generator to generate an integer:

```java
package com.packt.legacy.powermockito;

import java.util.Random;

public class MedicalBill {

  public static int generateId(){
    return new Random().nextInt();
  }
}
```

You cannot stub the `generateId()` method to return a hardcoded value, but the following `mockStatic()` method of PowerMockito allows us to stub the `generateId()` method to return a hardcoded value:

```java
package com.packt.legacy.powermockito;

import static org.junit.Assert.assertEquals;
import static org.powermock.api.mockito.PowerMockito.mockStatic;
import static org.powermock.api.mockito.PowerMockito.when;

import org.junit.Test;
import org.junit.runner.RunWith;
import org.powermock.core.classloader.annotations.PrepareForTest;
import org.powermock.modules.junit4.PowerMockRunner;

@RunWith(PowerMockRunner.class)
@PrepareForTest(MedicalBill.class)
public class StaticMethodTest {

  @Test
  public void stubs_static_methods() throws Exception {
    System.out.println(MedicalBill.generateId());
    //enable mocking
    mockStatic(MedicalBill.class);
    //stub the static method
    PowerMockito.when(MedicalBill.generateId()).thenReturn(1);
```

```
//check the stubbed value
assertEquals(1, MedicalBill.generateId());
    }
}
```

The test class is annotated with @RunWith(PowerMockRunner.class) and @PrepareForTest(MedicalBill.class), where PowerMockRunner bootstraps PowerMockito to use a classloader to load the classes, and @PrepareForTest enables the classes to be mocked.

The static mockStatic() method is defined in the org.powermock.api.mockito. PowerMockito class. This method allows us to mock static methods.

We need to mock static methods in the following circumstances:

- Code under test calls a utility class or a data access object with static methods, and static methods hide testing impediments, such as a database call, file access, and so on

- Code under test calls a third-party library; we cannot modify the third-party library source code, which in turn hides a testing impediment in a static method

Suppressing static blocks

Suppose legacy code has a static data initialization block and it loads a database driver in this block. If you need to unit test the class, you need to load the class and in turn, the static block is processed. So your test will indirectly load the database driver before executing a test. This is unacceptable, but you cannot suppress the static initialization using any mocking tool. PowerMockito allows us to suppress the static blocks and enables us to write test for the code that hides testing impediments in static initialization blocks.

The following class has a static block whereby it initializes a value with 100/0. This 100/0 signifies a testing impediment. If you load the class in a test harness, the test will fail with a divide by zero exception. Division by zero is just a trick to show the effect of the PowerMock @Suppress annotation and to state that the class does not work in functional mode:

```
public class StaticInitializationBlock {
  static int value;
  static{
    value = 100/0;
    System.out.println("In static block");
  }
}
```

The following PowerMockito test suppresses the static block:

```
package com.packt.legacy.powermockito;

import static org.junit.Assert.assertEquals;

import org.junit.Test;
import org.junit.runner.RunWith;
import org.powermock.core.classloader.annotations.
  SuppressStaticInitializationFor;
import org.powermock.modules.junit4.PowerMockRunner;

@RunWith(PowerMockRunner.class)
@SuppressStaticInitializationFor("com.packt.legacy.powermockito.St
  aticInitializationBlock")
public class StaticInitializationBlockTest {

  @Test
  public void supresses_static_initialization_blocks() {
    assertEquals(0,StaticInitializationBlock.value);
  }
}
```

In the preceding test, we assert `StaticInitializationBlock.`
`value` against `0` because `0` is the default value for an integer. The `@`
`SuppressStaticInitializationFor` annotation instructs the PowerMockito
classloader to skip the static initialization for the fully qualified class name.

Suppressing a superclass constructor

When a class needs to extend from another class in a third-party framework or
some other kind of module and the third-party class constructor hides a testing
impediment, then that prevents you from unit testing your own code. For example,
the framework may try to connect to the Internet to load some value or access
filesystem for some reason. You cannot suppress the super constructor chaining
from your unit test, and hence, your test may fail.

The following class has a constructor that hides a testing impediment; the divide by
zero replicates a testing impediment:

```
class DontExtendMePlease{
  DontExtendMePlease(){
    int x =1/0;
  }
}
```

The following class extends the `DontExtendMePlease` class:

```
public class SuppressSuperConstructor extends DontExtendMePlease{

  public SuppressSuperConstructor() {
    super();
  }

}
```

When we instantiate the `SuppressSuperConstructor` class in a test case, the test fails with the following error, to indicate that you cannot instantiate the class, as the super class constructor has some problem:

The PowerMockito JUnit test resolves the issue by suppressing the super class constructor:

```
import static org.powermock.api.support.membermodification.
  MemberMatcher.constructor;
import static org.powermock.api.support.membermodification.
  MemberModifier.suppress;

import org.junit.Test;
import org.junit.runner.RunWith;
import org.powermock.core.classloader.annotations.PrepareForTest;
import org.powermock.modules.junit4.PowerMockRunner;

@RunWith(PowerMockRunner.class)
@PrepareForTest(SuppressSuperConstructor.class)
public class SuppressSuperConstructorTest {

  @Test
```

```
    public void supresses_super_class_constructor() {
      suppress(constructor(DontExtendMePlease.class));
      new SuppressSuperConstructor();
      assertTrue("Just checking", true);
    }
  }
```

The `suppress` method takes a constructor or a field or a method. We are creating a constructor of the `DontExtendMePlease` class using the `constructor` (class) method. The PowerMockito classloader suppresses the constructor and allows us to unit test the code.

Suppressing our own constructor

Just like with the super class constructor, when we add our own constructor that hides a testing impediment, we cannot instantiate the class in test harness and hence, cannot unit test the class.

The following constructor divides by zero and indicates a testing impediment:

```
public class SuppressConstructor {

  public int someValue = 100;
  public SuppressConstructor(int val){
    val = val/0;
  }

}
```

However, PowerMock provides us a `Whitebox` class. It allows us to create class instances by suppressing the defined constructors; but the problem is that the values we initialize in the constructor are just ignored, or rather, not initialized. The following JUnit test uses `Whitebox` to suppress the parameterized constructor:

```
import static org.junit.Assert.assertNotNull;
import org.junit.Test;
import org.powermock.reflect.Whitebox;

public class SuppressConstructorTest {

  @Test
  public void supresses_own_constructor() throws Exception {
    SuppressConstructor nasty = Whitebox.newInstance(Suppress
      Constructor.class);
    assertNotNull(nasty);
  }
}
```

Suppressing methods

Sometimes, we need to suppress method calls. For instance, when our code under the test calls another method that hides a testing impediment, we must suppress the second method to proceed with the testing. Suppressing means the method will not be invoked; if a method returns a string (or any object) value, then a null value will be returned.

The following class has a private `getCurrency()` method; this method is called from the `format()` method:

```
package com.packt.legacy.powermockito;

public class SuppressMethod {

  public String format(String str){
    return str + getCurrency();
  }

  private String getCurrency(){
    return "$";
  }
}
```

The following JUnit will suppress the `getCurrency()` method call:

```
import static org.junit.Assert.assertFalse;
import static org.powermock.api.support.membermodification.
  MemberMatcher.method;
import static org.powermock.api.support.membermodification.
  MemberModifier.suppress;

import org.junit.Test;
import org.junit.runner.RunWith;
import org.powermock.core.classloader.annotations.PrepareForTest;
import org.powermock.modules.junit4.PowerMockRunner;

@RunWith(PowerMockRunner.class)
@PrepareForTest(SuppressMethod.class)
public class SuppressMethodTest {

  @Test
  public void supresses_method() throws Exception {
    suppress(method(SuppressMethod.class, "getCurrency"));
    SuppressMethod method = new SuppressMethod();
    assertFalse(method.format("10").contains("$"));
  }
}
```

Note that the `org.powermock.api.support.membermodification.` `MemberModifier.suppress` method takes `org.powermock.api.support.` `membermodification.MemberMatcher.method`, the method that has to be suppressed. We passed the class and the method name `getCurrency`. Spell the method name correctly (because it is passed as a string) and without parenthesis. An immediate call to the `getCurrency()` method from the `format()` method is suppressed.

Stubbing private methods

You cannot access private methods of a class from outside the class. When a private method hides a testing impediment, and that method is invoked from a public or protected method, then you cannot JUnit test the public/protected method as you cannot bypass the private method call or stub the private method. However, PowerMockito allows us to stub private methods and enables us to write JUnit tests by suppressing the testing impediments.

The following example has a private method known as `secretValue()`; this method returns a secret value and the other public method `exposeTheSecretValue()` calls the `secretValue()` method. When we call the `exposeTheSecretValue()` method from a JUnit test, it always returns the same secret value, but if we need to change the `secretValue()` method for every method call, then we need to stub the private method's behavior:

```
package com.packt.legacy.powermockito;

public class PrivateMethod {

  private String secretValue(){
    return "#$$%^&*";
  }

  public String exposeTheSecretValue(){
    return secretValue();
  }
}
```

To stub the private method using PowerMockito, we need to create a spy object of the class and then stub the private method on the spy object. Remember that we cannot access a `private` method from outside the class; so when we stub a private method, we just pass the method name as a string value. We cannot call the method directly as its access scope is private. Hence, the name is passed as a string so that, using reflection, the method is found and stubbed. Make sure you spell the method name correctly. The following test exhibits the `private` method's stubbing:

```
package com.packt.legacy.powermockito;

import static org.junit.Assert.*;
import static org.powermock.api.mockito.PowerMockito.*;

import org.junit.Test;
import org.junit.runner.RunWith;
import org.powermock.core.classloader.annotations.PrepareForTest;
import org.powermock.modules.junit4.PowerMockRunner;

@RunWith(PowerMockRunner.class)
@PrepareForTest(PrivateMethod.class)
public class PrivateMethodTest {

  @Test
  public void stubs_private_methods() throws Exception {
    PrivateMethod privateMethodClass = spy(new PrivateMethod());
    when(privateMethodClass, "secretValue").thenReturn("123");

assertEquals("123", privateMethodClass.exposeTheSecretValue());
  }
}
```

The test stubs the `secretValue` method to return `123` and asserts the value by invoking the public method `exposeTheSecretValue`.

Stubbing final methods

Mockito cannot stub final methods, as Java doesn't allow us to override the final methods. However, when a final method hides a testing impediment, either we cannot unit test the method, or remove the final keyword and override the method for JUnit testing. This actually violates the encapsulation principle, but the good news is that PowerMockito allows us to stub the final methods.

The following example demonstrates the `final` method's stubbing:

```
package com.packt.legacy.powermockito;

public class FinalMethod {

  public final String getValue(){
    return null;
  }
}
```

The `getValue()` method is a final method, but we can mock the class and stub the final method using the `@PrepareForTest` annotation. The following JUnit test stubs the `getValue()` method:

```
@RunWith(PowerMockRunner.class)
@PrepareForTest(FinalMethod.class)
public class FinalMethodTest {

  private static final String A_STUBBED_VALUE = "A stubbed value";

  @Test
  public void stubs_final_methods() throws Exception {
    FinalMethod finalMethod = mock(FinalMethod.class);
    when(finalMethod.getValue()).thenReturn(A_STUBBED_VALUE);
    assertEquals(A_STUBBED_VALUE, finalMethod.getValue());
  }
}
```

Mocking final classes

You cannot extend a final class, but during JUnit testing, we encounter that third-party framework classes or external module classes are final and they hide testing impediments, but we cannot change the files as we don't have the permission to change the source code to make them nonfinal classes. Luckily, PowerMockito allows us to mock final classes. The following example will work with a final class:

```
public final class SystemVerifier {
  public boolean isInstallable(){
    return false;
  }
}
```

The `SystemVerifier` class is a final class and it has a public method `isInstallable()`; this method checks system prerequisites, such as RAM, disk space, and so on. If everything is okay, then returns `true`; we are hardcoding the method to return `false`.

The `SoftwareInstaller` class has a reference to the `SystemVerifier` class. When the `SystemVerifier.isInstallable` method returns `true`, it starts installing a software. The following is the `SoftwareInstaller` class:

```
public class SoftwareInstaller {
  private final SystemVerifier systemVerifier;

  public SoftwareInstaller(SystemVerifier systemVerifier) {
    this.systemVerifier = systemVerifier;
  }

  public boolean install(String packageName) {
    if (systemVerifier.isInstallable()) {
      // install something
      return true;
    }

    return false;
  }
}
```

We have already hardcoded the `isInstallable()` method to return `false`; to unit test the installation part, we need to stub the `isInstallable()` method to return `true`, but the `SystemVerifier` class is a final class, so we cannot stub the method.

The following PowerMockito JUnit test mocks the final class `SystemVerifier` and stubs the `isInstallable()` method to return `true`:

```
@RunWith(PowerMockRunner.class)
@PrepareForTest(SystemVerifier.class)
public class FinalClassTest {

  @Test
  public void mocks_final_classes() throws Exception {
    SystemVerifier systemVerifier = mock(SystemVerifier.class);
    when(systemVerifier.isInstallable()).thenReturn(true);

    SoftwareInstaller installer = new SoftwareInstaller
      (systemVerifier);
    assertTrue(installer.install("java"));
  }
}
```

Designing for testability with Mockito

We learned about testing impediments and how to refactor them. We cannot unit test code when testing impediments are present; we refactor code and move the impediments out (to another class or method), and during testing, the impediments are replaced with mock objects. PowerMock is a dirty solution and it should only be used for legacy code. This is the better way is to refactor the source and make more test friendly.

However, sometimes we cannot mock out the external dependencies due to testing-unfriendly design. This section covers the design for testability, or rather, things to avoid in code. The following Java constructs go up against mocking the testing impediments:

- Constructors initialize testing impediments
- Class level variable declaration and initialization
- Private methods
- Final methods
- Static methods
- Final classes
- Use of *new*
- Static variable declaration and initialization
- Static initialization blocks

You cannot unit test legacy code because it is either tightly coupled, or testing unfavorable language constructs hide the testing impediments. The following section explains testing unfavorable constructs.

To represent a testing impediment, we'll throw a special runtime exception `TestingImpedimentException`. If your test fails with a `TestingImpedimentException` error, it means you cannot automate the test, as your code has testing unfavorable features.

Identifying constructor issues

To build a test, we need to instantiate the class in test harness, but the problem with legacy code is that it is difficult to break dependency and instantiate a class in a test harness. For example, in a constructor, the class instantiates many objects, reads from the `properties` file, or even creates a database connection. There could be many callers of the class, so you cannot change the constructor to pass dependencies, otherwise it will cause a series of compilation errors.

We will take a look at the legacy code and try to write a test for the class.

Suppose we have a `TestingUnfavorableConstructor` class with two external dependencies, `DatabaseDependency` and `FileReadDependency`. Both the dependencies are slow in nature and testing impediments. The `TestingUnfavorableConstructor` class creates dependencies in the constructor. The dependencies represent the database access and the file reads from the `TestingUnfavorableConstructor` constructor. The following is the class:

```java
public class TestingUnfavorableConstructor {
  private DatabaseDependency dependency1;
  private FileReadDependency dependency2;

  public TestingUnfavorableConstructor() {
    this.dependency1 = new DatabaseDependency();
    this.dependency2 = new FileReadDependency();
  }

  public Object testMe(Object arg) {
    return arg;
  }

}
```

If we want to unit test the `testMe()` behavior of the class, we need to create an object for the `TestingUnfavorableConstructor` class. However, when we try to create an instant in the unit test, the class fails to indicate that the class cannot be instantiated from an automated test suite. The following is the output:

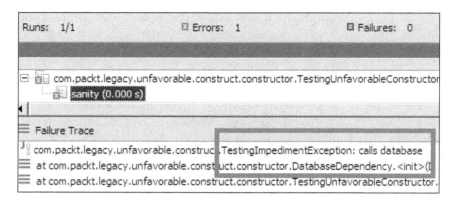

To overcome this, you should inject the dependencies through the constructor instead of creating them in the constructor.

We cannot modify the default constructor because the class is invoked from many other clients; we cannot break the clients. Two other options are as follows:

- Keep the default constructor as it is, create another constructor, and inject dependencies through this new constructor. From test, we can call this new constructor. You're also putting the code into production for testing purpose; this is a test smell, but to overcome this, you need to unit test the code with PowerMock.

- Create a protected method, move the dependency instantiation to that method, create two setter methods, and initialize the dependencies through a setter injection. In the test, create a fake object for the main class, override the protected method to do nothing, and pass the dependencies through setter methods.

The first option is relatively straightforward; we'll apply the second approach.

The following is the modified code:

```
public class TestingUnfavorableConstructor {
  private DatabaseDependency dependency1;
  private FileReadDependency dependency2;

  public TestingUnfavorableConstructor() {
    createDependencies();
```

```
    }

    protected void createDependencies() {
      this.dependency1 = new DatabaseDependency();
      this.dependency2 = new FileReadDependency();
    }

    public void setDependency1(DatabaseDependency dependency1) {
      this.dependency1 = dependency1;
    }

    public void setDependency2(FileReadDependency dependency2) {
      this.dependency2 = dependency2;
    }

    public Object testMe(Object arg) {
      return arg;
    }
  }
```

The following unit test overrides the `TestingUnfavorableConstructor` class, provides an empty implementation of the `createDependencies()` method, creates mock dependencies, and calls setter methods to set the mock dependencies:

```
  @RunWith(MockitoJUnitRunner.class)
  public class TestingUnfavorableConstructorTest {
    @Mock DatabaseDependency dep1;
    @Mock FileReadDependency dep2;
    TestingUnfavorableConstructor unfavorableConstructor;
    @Before  public void setUp() {
      unfavorableConstructor= new TestingUnfavorableConstructor() {
        protected void createDependencies() {
        }
      };

      unfavorableConstructor.setDependency1(dep1);
      unfavorableConstructor.setDependency2(dep2);
    }

    @Test    public void sanity() throws Exception {
    }
  }
```

The empty test method is used to check the health of the test setup, as you need at least one test method to invoke the setup method.

> Do not instantiate dependencies in the constructor; the dependencies may exhibit testing impediments and make the class nontestable. Instead of instantiating the dependencies in the constructor, you can pass the real implementations (real dependencies) to the constructor or setter method of the code under the test.

Realizing initialization issues

Declaring the class-level variable and instantiating the object at the same time creates a problem; you don't get a chance to mock out the variable. The following example explains the problem.

The `VariableInitialization` class has a database dependency and the dependency is instantiated where it is declared:

```
Public class VariableInitialization {
    DatabaseDependency dependency1 = new DatabaseDependency();
    public void testMe(Object obj) {

    }
}
```

When you instantiate the `VariableInitialization` class in the test, the test fails. The following screenshot shows the output:

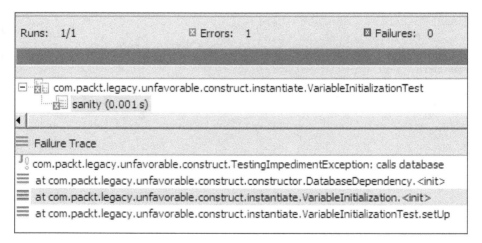

Here is the test class:

```
public class VariableInitializationTest {
  VariableInitialization initialization;

  @Before public void setUp() throws Exception {
    initialization = new VariableInitialization();
  }
  @Test    public void sanity() throws Exception {
  }
}
```

The following are the options to overcome class-level variable initialization:

- Add a default constructor and move the dependency instantiation to the default constructor, create another constructor, and inject dependencies through this new constructor. From the test, we can call this new constructor. This is a test smell, as the code is added in production for testing purposes.

- Add a default constructor, move the dependency instantiation to a protected method, call the method from the default constructor, create a setter method, and initialize the dependency through a setter injection. In the test, create a fake object of the main class and override the protected method to do nothing, and pass the dependencies through the setter methods.

 Do not instantiate the testing impediment variables at the class level. You can still instantiate variables, such as list = new ArrayList<String>() and more, which are totally reasonable to build internal fields in themselves; it's the difference between coupling to collaborating classes and the internal state.

Working with private methods

Private methods are useful for hiding the internal state and encapsulation, but they can also hide the testing impediments. The following example explains the details.

The PrivateMethod class has a private method showError(). This private method hides a test impediment. When we unit test the validate() method with a null object, the validate() method calls the showError message:

```
public class PrivateMethod {
  public Object validate(Object arg) {
    if(arg == null) {
      showError("Null input");
```

```
    }
    return arg;
  }

  private void showError(String msg) {
    GraphicalInterface.showMessage(msg);
  }
}
```

The following is the test output:

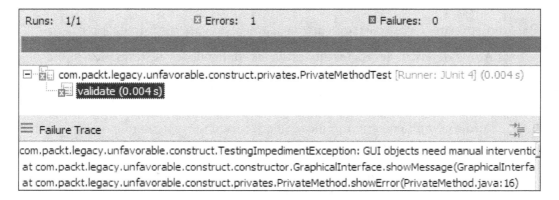

You can extract the testing impediments to a protected (or default package visibility) method, or you can separate the concern, create a new class, move the testing impediment to that class, and inject the new class as a dependency. Objects should do one thing; if you've got a method you want to test that does X and is in the same class as a method that does Y (which is so totally different that it can't be allowed to happen in your test for X), then your class must be doing two things. Split these responsibilities.

In this example, validating objects and showing errors are two different responsibilities and should be managed by two different classes.

[Do not hide testing impediments in private methods.]

The following code refactors the testing impediments and makes the class unit testable:

```
public class PrivateMethodRefactored {
  public Object validate(Object arg) {
    if(arg == null) {
      showError("Null input");
    }

    return arg;
  }

  protected void showError(String msg) {
    GraphicalInterface.showMessage(msg);
  }
}
```

The showError method's access specifier is changed to protected.

The following test code extends the class with an anonymous implementation and overrides the protected method with an empty implementation. The test code invokes the validate() method on the new anonymous implementation of the PrivateMethodRefactored class, and in turn, the polymorphic behavior calls the empty implementation. Hence, the test will always bypass the testing impediments by calling the overridden empty implementation of the testing impediment, but the real production code will always invoke the protected method.

```
public class PrivateMethodRefactoredTest {

  PrivateMethodRefactored privateMethod;

  @Before
  public void setUp() {
    privateMethod = new PrivateMethodRefactored() {
      protected void showError(String msg) {

      }
    };
  }

  @Test
  public void validate() throws Exception {
    privateMethod.validate(null);
  }
}
```

This approach of bypassing the testing impediments with overridden versions of the testing impediments is known as **faking** or **fake object**. If the code under the test contains many testing impediments, it is not possible to override all of them in an anonymous class; rather, we can create an inner class, extend the code under test, and override all testing-unfriendly methods.

Working with final methods

When a method is final, you cannot override it. If the final method hides any testing impediment, you cannot unit test the class. The following example demonstrates the issue.

The FinalDependency class has a final method called doSomething. This method hides a testing-unfriendly feature. The following is the class definition:

```
public class FinalDependency {

  public final void doSomething() {
    throw new TestingImpedimentException("Final methods cannot be
      overriden");
  }
}
```

The FinalMethodDependency class has a dependency on FinalDependency, and in the testMe method, it calls the doSomething method:

```
public class FinalMethodDependency {

  private final FinalDependency dependency;

  public FinalMethodDependency(FinalDependency dependency) {
    this.dependency = dependency;
  }
  public void testMe() {
    dependency.doSomething();
  }
}
```

In the test, we'll mock the dependency and unit test the code:

```
@RunWith(MockitoJUnitRunner.class)
public class FinalMethodDependencyTest {
  @Mock
  FinalDependency finalDependency;
  FinalMethodDependency methodDependency;
```

```
  @Before
  public void setUp() {
    methodDependency = new FinalMethodDependency(finalDependency);
  }
@Test
  public void testSomething() throws Exception {
    methodDependency.testMe();
  }
}
```

When we run the test, it still accesses the testing impediment, as the mock object cannot stub a final method. When we try to stub the method, we get an error. The following test stubs the final method call:

```
@Test
public void testSomething() throws Exception {
  doNothing().when(finalDependency).doSomething();
  methodDependency.testMe();
}
```

When we run the test, we get the following error message thrown by the Mockito framework:

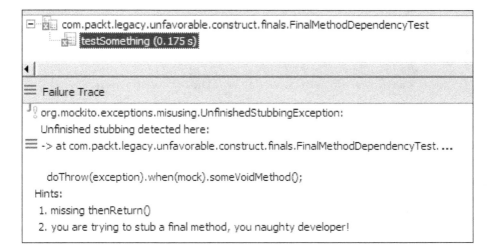

 Do not hide the testing impediments in the final methods; you cannot override or stub a final method.

A possible way to overcome this is by extracting the content of the final method to a protected method, calling the protected method from the final method, and overriding the protected method in the test. If you cannot touch the class at all, use the PowerMock framework. For example, when you have only a JAR file, create a `MethodDependency` interface with `FinalDependency`, implementing it as we have done here, rather than having `FindalMethodDependency` depend on `MethodDependency`. Then in production, you need to provide a `FinalMethodDependency` instance (as done here), but in tests, you can stub the interface happily, which doesn't have any final methods, and you are all set to proceed.

Exploring static method issues

Static methods are good for utility classes but unnecessary use of static can hide the testing impediments and create a problem for unit testing. The following example demonstrates the issue.

The `SingletonDependency` class is an implementation of the **Gang of Four (GoF)** singleton design pattern. It has a private constructor and a static `getInstance()` method to create only a single instance of the class. The static `callMe()` method hides a testing impediment. Note that the GoF singleton pattern doesn't define methods as static, but in this example, we are defining the `callMe()` method as static, to display a drawback of static methods. The following is the singleton implementation:

```java
public class SingletonDependency {
  private static SingletonDependency singletonDependency;

  private SingletonDependency() {
  }

  public synchronized static SingletonDependency getInstance() {
    if (singletonDependency == null) {
      singletonDependency = new SingletonDependency();
    }

    return singletonDependency;
  }

  Public static void callMe() {
    throw new TestingImpedimentException("we dont need
      singleton");
  }
}
```

The `VictimOfAPatternLover` class has a dependency on `SingletonDependency`.
The following are the class details:

```java
public class VictimOfAPatternLover {
  private final SingletonDependency dependency;

  public VictimOfAPatternLover(SingletonDependency dependency) {
    this.dependency = dependency;
  }

  public void testMe() {
    dependency.callMe();
  }
}
```

Mockito cannot stub a static method. When we try to stub the static `callMe()`
method, it still calls the original method and fails for the testing impediment.
You cannot stub a static method.

 Do not hide the testing impediments in static methods; you cannot
stub static methods.

The only way to overcome this issue is to create a protected method and wrap the
static call. From the code, call the wrapped method, and from the test, override the
protected method. We will now add a wrapper method in the dependency class and
call the static method from it:

```java
public static void callMe() {
  throw new TestingImpedimentException("Come on we dont need
    singleton");
}

protected void wrapper() {
  callMe();
}
}
```

From the code, call the wrapper method:

```java
public void testMe() {
  dependency.wrapper();
}
```

Stub the wrapper method in the test:

```
@Test
  public void testMe() throws Exception {
    Mockito.doNothing().when(dependency).wrapper();
    aPatternLover.testMe();
  }
```

The better way to do this is to stop calling the static method from this class entirely and wrap it in a separate class, which you pass in as a dependency.

Say you've got a `Database.create()` static method you call from your class A. You could have a `DatabaseBuilder` class which you pass into class A, and then just have a call `databaseBuilder.create()`, where `DatabaseBuilder` is something like the following:

```
public class DatabaseBuilder {
  public void create() {
    Database.create();
  }
}
```

And then in the tests, you just provide a stubbed database builder and swap out the whole thing. I would really not recommend using this pattern of making private methods protected and overriding them, except where it's absolutely necessary.

Alternatively, of course, if you can't change the API; you'd use PowerMock to stub the static call.

Working with final classes

You cannot override a final class, so you can hide testing-unfavorable features in a final class. The following example explains the problem.

The final class hides a testing impediment:

```
public final class FinalDepencyClass {

  public void poison() {
    throw new TestingImpedimentException("Finals cannot be
      mocked");
  }
}
```

The code under the test has a dependency on the final class:

```
public class FinalClassDependency {
  private final FinalDepencyClass finalDepencyClass;

  public FinalClassDependency(FinalDepencyClass finalDepencyClass)
    {
    this.finalDepencyClass = finalDepencyClass;
  }

  public void testMe() {
    finalDepencyClass.poison();
  }
}
```

In the test, we'll try to stub the `poison` method:

```
@RunWith(MockitoJUnitRunner.class)
public class FinalClassDependencyTest {
  @Mock
  FinalDepencyClass finalDependency;

  FinalClassDependency test;

  @Before
  public void setUp() {
    test = new FinalClassDependency(finalDependency);
  }
  @Test
  public void testMe() throws Exception {
    Mockito.doNothing().when(finalDependency).poison();
    test.testMe();
  }
}
```

The test fails with a `MockitoException` error as Mockito cannot mock a final class. The following screenshot displays the JUnit output:

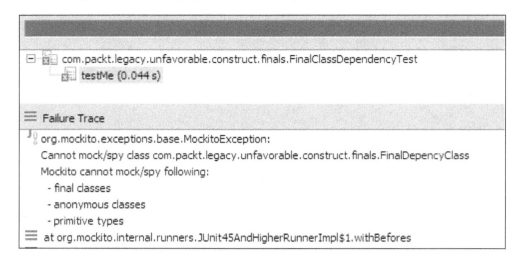

 Do not hide the testing impediments in final classes; you cannot mock a final class.

Final classes are important for framework or architecture design so that no one can hack the behavior, but it can create a serious problem for unit testing. Before you choose to make a class final, ensure that your final class is a final implementation of some interface so that other clients of the class can potentially use stubbed instances of the interface.

Learning new concerns

Java instantiates classes using the `new` operator, but an innocent *new* can create a problem for unit testing.

The following example explains the issue. The `PoisonIvy` constructor has a testing impediment, for instance, when the method call fetches data from a database table or reads from the filesystem, we represent the testing impediment with the `TestingImpedimentException` error:

```
public class PoisonIvy {

  public PoisonIvy() {
    throw new TestingImpedimentException("use dependency
      injection");
```

```
    }

    public void poison() {

    }
}
```

The following is the code that calls the `PoisonIvy` class:

```
public class NewExpressionDependency {

    public void testMe() {
        PoisonIvy ivy = new PoisonIvy();
        ivy.poison();
    }
}
```

When we unit test the `testMe()` code, it fails. The `testMe()` method directly creates an instance of dependency and calls the `poison()` method. You cannot override this new expression. If we want to unit test the `testMe()` method, first we need to move the `new` operator outside `testMe()`, as we cannot instantiate the `PoisonIvy` class. The constructor of the `PoisonIvy` class throws an exception, hence we cannot unit test the `testMe` behavior unless we move the object creation out of `testMe`. Instead of creating a new instance of `PoisonIvy` inside `testMe()`, we can pass an instance of `PoisonIvy` as a method argument, or create a class-level dependency and pass `PoisonIvy` as a constructor- or setter-dependency argument.

Program to an interface, not an implementation. Rather than hardcoding the collaborator instantiation of the subtype into the code, assign the concrete collaborator implementation object through a dependency injection. Separate the parts of the codebase that use objects, and implement your logic from the parts that decide which objects to use where (typically with a DI framework such as Guice or Spring).

What does *program to an interface, not an implementation* mean? It means, program to a super type, rather than a subtype. You can interchange the implementation at runtime. In a collection framework, we have the `List` interface and its many implementations. In your class, always define a variable or method return type for `List` not `ArrayList`, so that if required, you can assign any implementation you want.

In this example, you can pass the `PoisonIvy` class as a constructor or setter dependency, and at runtime (during testing), you can pass a mock or a fake implementation to suppress the testing impediments.

Exploring static variables and blocks

Static initializations and static blocks are executed during class loading; you cannot override them. If you initialize a testing impediment in a static block, you cannot unit test the class. The following example demonstrates the issue.

The StaticBlockOwner class has a static variable known as StaticBlockDependency, and it initializes the variable in a static block. The following is the class:

```
public class StaticBlockOwner {
  private static StaticBlockDependency blockDependency;
  static {
    blockDependency = new StaticBlockDependency();
    blockDependency.loadTime = new Date();
  }
  public void testMe() {
  }
}
```

When we unit test the class, it fails. The following is the unit test:

```
public class StaticBlockOwnerTest {
  StaticBlockOwner owner;
  @Before public void setUp()  {
    owner = new StaticBlockOwner();
  }
  @Test    public void clean() throws Exception {
    owner.testMe();
  }
}
```

The test fails with java.lang.ExceptionInInitializationError as it tries to instantiate the dependency in a static block and the dependency throws an exception.

Do not instantiate dependencies in a static block. You cannot override the testing impediments; you shouldn't be using static initializer blocks at all.

Summary

This chapter covered legacy code, testing impediments, design for testability, and unit testing the legacy code with Mockito and PowerMock.

Now you should be able to write JUnit tests for legacy code with Mockito and PowerMock, refactor legacy code to make it unit testable, and design code to bypass the testing impediments.

The next chapter, *Developing SOA with Mockito*, will cover **Service-oriented Architecture (SOA)**, web services, and how to unit test the REST- and SOAP-based web services with Mockito.

6

Developing SOA with Mockito

"The Web as I envisaged it, we have not seen it yet. The future is still so much bigger than the past."

– Tim Berners-Lee

This chapter explores web services, web service styles—SOAP-based and RESTful, web service components, and building and unit testing SOAP and RESTful web services with Mockito.

Exploring Service-oriented Architecture (SOA)

Service-oriented Architecture (SOA) is an architectural style that transforms business use cases into a set of interlinked services or reusable business tasks that can be accessed over a network. This could be an intranet or over the Internet. The services could be geographically and technologically diverse. SOA can combine services hosted on remote locations as if they are hosted on your local machine, and accomplish a specific business task, enabling your business to quickly adapt to changing conditions and requirements.

Service is a self-contained unit of business tasks, such as a credit card payment or stock quote. SOA orchestrates the services to accomplish a bigger task. The main theme of SOA is loose coupling so that you can reuse the services, for instance, define fine-grained services and combine them in a coarse-grained service.

Organizations can have existing heterogeneous IT systems, such as a payroll system developed in C++ and an expense claim workflow developed in Java. SOA enables businesses to leverage existing investments, by allowing them to reuse existing IT systems, and accomplishes interoperability between heterogeneous applications and technologies.

For more details on SOA, you can visit `http://www.oracle.com/technetwork/articles/javase/soa-142870.html` or the book *Applied SOA: Service-oriented Architecture and Design Strategies*.

SOA can rely on web services for interoperability between heterogeneous applications and technologies. In the next section, we'll explore the web services.

Working with web services

Organizations rely on different software applications, each with their own business purpose. These different software applications run on different platforms and operating systems, and are implemented in different programming languages. So, it is very difficult for different applications to communicate with each other and share their resources in a coordinated way. Heterogeneous applications can communicate with each other via web services. The following are the web service characteristics:

- Web services are web application components
- Web services communicate using open standards, such as XML, SOAP, and HTTP
- Web services are self-contained and self-describing
- HTTP and XML are the basis for web services

Web services are client and server applications that communicate over **HyperText Transfer Protocol (HTTP)** and provide a standard means for interoperating between software applications running on a variety of platforms and frameworks. Web services are characterized by interoperability and extensibility.

We'll be looking at two of the most common tools for building web services in Java, namely, the **Java API for XML Web Services (JAX-WS)** and **Java API for RESTful Web Services (JAX-RS)**:

- **JAX-WS**: This uses XML messages that follow the client-to-server communication that is done through messages the **Simple Object Access Protocol (SOAP)** standard. The SOAP message architecture and message formats are defined in XML. Each web service operation has a machine-readable description written in the **Web Services Description Language (WSDL)**, which is an XML format for defining interfaces syntactically.

- **JAX-RS**: This provides the functionality for **Representational State Transfer (RESTful)** web services. REST is well suited for basic, ad hoc integration scenarios. RESTful web services are better integrated with HTTP than SOAP-based services. REST web services do not require XML messages or WSDL service-API definitions. **JavaScript Object Notation (JSON)** is typically the XML alternative of choice for all data transfer that is required in RESTful web services.

Visit the following URL for more details on JAX-WS and JAX-RS:

```
http://docs.oracle.com/javaee/6/tutorial/doc/gijti.html
```

In the following section, we'll explore the JAX-WS web services with Eclipse.

Exploring JAX-WS with Eclipse

JAX-WS web services require a service description written in WSDL.

A WSDL document defines services as collections of network endpoints or ports. In WSDL, the abstract definition of endpoints and messages is separated from their concrete network deployment or data format bindings. This allows the reuse of abstract definitions: messages, which are abstract descriptions of the data being exchanged and port types, which are abstract collections of operations.

A WSDL document uses the following elements in the definition of network services:

- **Types**: This is a container for data type definitions (such as XSD or schemas).
- **Message**: This is an abstract, typed definition of the data being communicated.
- **Operation**: This is an abstract description of an action supported by the service.
- **Port type**: This is an abstract set of operations supported by one or more endpoints.
- **Port**: This is a single endpoint defined as a combination of a binding and a network address.
- **Binding**: This is a concrete protocol and data format specification for a particular port type. The binding is usually SOAP, and the encoding and data formatting regulations used (also known as the style) are usually literal (this includes document/literal, and sometimes RPC/literal).
- **Service**: This is a collection of related endpoints.

JAX-WS web services can be developed using two approaches:

- **Top-down approach or contract-first web services**: In this, Schema/XSD, WSDL, and message formats are defined; and then, using tools, the Java service skeletons are generated
- **Bottom-up approach or contract-last web services**: The Java services are developed first, then using tools/wizards, the WSDL and the web service are created from the Java classes

In this section, we'll follow the bottom-up approach.

To develop a web service in Eclipse, the following components should be installed on your machine:

- You need Apache Tomcat, and you can visit the Tomcat website for installation and setup instructions; the URL is `http://tomcat.apache.org/`.
- Your Eclipse should have the web tool platform component installed. You can go to the **About Eclipse** menu and click on the **Installation Details** button for details on the WTP components, under the **Plug-ins** tab. The following is the screenshot of the installation details. For details on Eclipse, visit `http://www.eclipse.org/webtools/`.

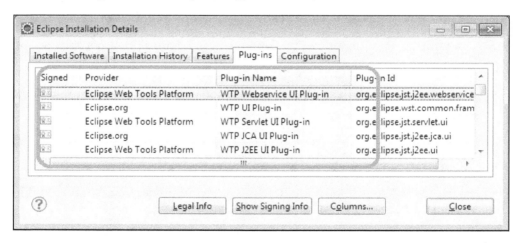

The following are steps to create a web service with Apache Axis and
Apache Tomcat:

1. Create a dynamic web project in Eclipse and enter the project name
   as DNACheckWS.

2. We'll create a DNA fingerprint service to verify a DNA sample with the
   existing database for a match. The DNA sample will hold a DNA profile of
   DNA elements, each element will have a genetic marker, such as TH01, and
   corresponding allele A and allele B values such as TH01, 8, and 11. The
   DNA profile will be examined against the database, and if the exact match is
   found, the person's details will be sent back as a response.

3. Create a ProfileElement class in the com.packt.webservice.jaxws.dto
   package, add three string attributes geneticMarker, alleleA, and alleleB,
   and generate getters and setters for the three attributes. The following is the
   code for the class details:

```
package com.packt.webservice.jaxws.dto;

public class ProfileElement {
  private String geneticMarker;
  private String alleleA;
  private String alleleB;
  //The getters and setters are ignored for brevity
}
```

4. Create a DNAProfile class with an array of ProfileElements. The following
   is the code for the class details:

```
package com.packt.webservice.jaxws.dto;

public class DNAProfile {
  private ProfileElement[] dnaElements;
  //The getters and setters are ignored for brevity
}
```

5. Create an empty service DNAFingerPrintService for matching a DNA
   profile with an existing set of DNAs; it just returns a fixed value here.
   The following are the details:

```
package com.packt.webservice.jaxws.service;

import com.packt.webservice.jaxws.dto.DNAProfile;

public class DNAFingerPrintService {
  public String findMatch(DNAProfile dnaProfile){

    return "sujoy";
  }
}
```

6. We'll create a web service out of `DNAFingerPrintService` with runtime Axis and Tomcat. Right-click on the project and select the **Web Services** menu, expand the menu, and select **Create Web Service**. The following screenshot displays the steps:

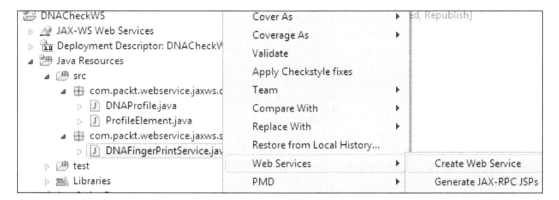

7. A wizard will open; select the web service type as **Bottom up Java bean Web Service** and choose the server runtime as Tomcat and the web service runtime as Apache Axis. You can deploy the web service to IBM WebSphere or choose the web service runtime as Apache CFX, as shown in the following screenshot:

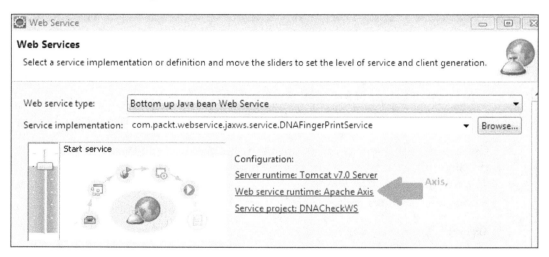

Do not generate the client; set the slider to **No client**:

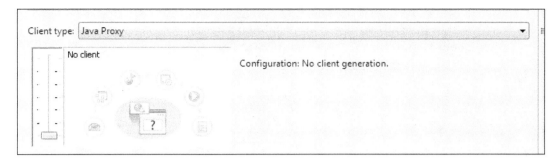

8. In the next section, select the `findMatch` method, select the **Style and use** option as **document/literal (wrapped)**, and hit the **Next** or **Finish** button:

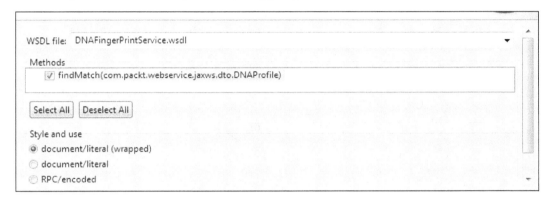

9. You can see that the following files are newly generated. These are required for the server to run the web service and deploy the module into the web server container. The most important file created here is **DNAFingerPrintService.wsdl**:

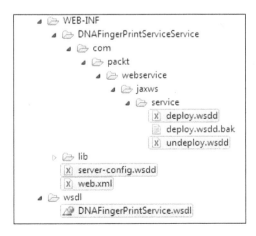

10. Click on **DNAFingerPrintService.wsdl** and open it in the Eclipse editor; check that the web service URL is defined as `http://localhost:8080/DNACheckWS/services/DNAFingerPrintService`:

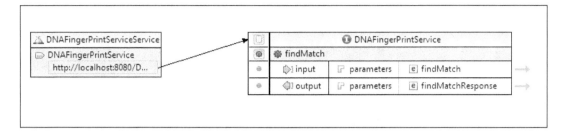

11. Deploy the project in Tomcat, right-click on the project, and select **Run on Server**. Once the server is started, open a web browser and type the following URL to verify that the web service is deployed:

    `http://localhost:8080/DNACheckWS/services/`
    `DNAFingerPrintService?wsdl`

    The following is the WSDL output:

```
<wsdl:definitions targetNamespace="http://service.jaxws.webservice.packt.com"
  xmlns:impl="http://service.jaxws.webservice.packt.com"
  xmlns:wsdl="http://schemas.xmlsoap.org/wsdl/"
  <!--
    WSDL created by Apache Axis version: 1.4
    Built on Apr 22, 2006 (06:55:48 PDT)
  -->
  <wsdl:types>
  + <schema elementFormDefault="qualified" targetNamespace="http://service.jaxws.webservice.packt.com"
  + <schema elementFormDefault="qualified" targetNamespace="http://dto.jaxws.webservice.packt.com"
    </wsdl:types>
+ <wsdl:message name="findMatchRequest">
+ <wsdl:message name="findMatchResponse">
+ <wsdl:portType name="DNAFingerPrintService">
+ <wsdl:binding name="DNAFingerPrintServiceSoapBinding" type="impl:DNAFingerPrintService">
  <wsdl:service name="DNAFingerPrintServiceService">
  - <wsdl:port binding="impl:DNAFingerPrintServiceSoapBinding" name="DNAFingerPrintService">
      <wsdlsoap:address location="http://localhost:8080/DNACheckWS/services/DNAFingerPrintService" />
    </wsdl:port>
  </wsdl:service>
</wsdl:definitions>
```

We're done with the web service server component; next we'll build the client component to invoke the web service:

1. Create a Java project DNAWsClient.

2. We'll generate the client stubs from the web service and, in turn, it will create the remote interface to call the business methods, namely, a server proxy class (the intermediate between the client and the server) and a service locator class (contains the details of the server). However, to generate the client stub, we need a wsdl file. Copy the wsdl folder from the DNACheckWS project's WebContent folder to the DNAWsClient project's src folder, as shown in the following screenshot:

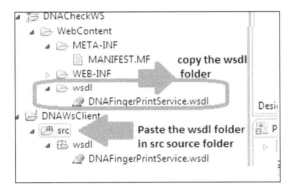

3. Right-click on the wsdl file and select **Web Services | Generate Client**, as shown in the following screenshot:

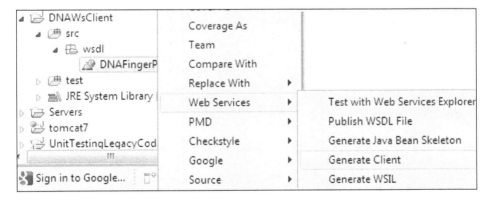

4. The Eclipse plugin will generate the `dto` classes and stubs. The following are the generated classes:

5. Now create a client class named `DNAFingerPrintWsInvoker` to invoke the web service. The `DNAFingerPrintServiceServiceLocator` class is a facade class and it hides the underlying service invocation details. We'll create a `findMatch` method to invoke the web service and return the result. The following is the client code:

```
package com.packt.webservice.jaxws.client;

import java.rmi.RemoteException;

import javax.xml.rpc.ServiceException;

import com.packt.webservice.jaxws.dto.DNAProfile;
import com.packt.webservice.jaxws.service.DNAFinger
  PrintServiceServiceLocator;

public class DNAFingerPrintWsInvoker {

  public String findMatch(DNAProfile dnaProfile) throws
    RemoteException, ServiceException {
  DNAFingerPrintServiceServiceLocator locator = new
    DNAFingerPrintServiceServiceLocator();
  return locator.getDNAFingerPrintService().findMatch
    (dnaProfile);
  }

}
```

6. Our client code is ready for testing, but to JUnit test the web service call, we need to refactor the code, as the findMatch method instantiates the DNAFingerPrintServiceServiceLocator class and delegates call to the locator for accessing the web service. The DNAFingerPrintServiceServiceLocator class makes a network call and, hence, it can be considered as a testing impediment. We need to bypass the instantiation of the testing impediments, to make our test reliable, with a mock object. Add Mockito and JUnit JAR files to the project's classpath and create a test class DNAFingerPrintWsInvokerTest under the test source package.

7. Refactor the DNAFingerPrintWsInvoker class and extract a protected method getServiceLocator() to return a new instance of the DNAFingerPrintServiceServiceLocator class. Replace the new DNAFingerPrintServiceServiceLocator() call with the getServiceLocator() call. The following code shows the modified class. Also, as a better alternative, DNAFinderPrintWsInvoker could take a DNAFingerPrintServiceServiceLocation call as a constructor argument, which is to be provided by whoever uses it. The tests can then provide a stub to that constructor. This reduces coupling between the test and the class under the test's internals and ensures that we're actually definitely testing the code, which is as close as possible to what's going to be running in production:

```
public class DNAFingerPrintWsInvoker {

    public String findMatch(DNAProfile dnaProfile) throws
        RemoteException, ServiceException {
        return getServiceLocator().getDNAFingerPrintService()
            .findMatch(dnaProfile);
    }

    protected DNAFingerPrintServiceServiceLocator
        getServiceLocator() {
        return new DNAFingerPrintServiceServiceLocator();
    }

}
```

8. Modify the test as follows:

```
@RunWith(MockitoJUnitRunner.class)
public class DNAFingerPrintWsInvokerTest {

    DNAFingerPrintWsInvoker invoker;
    @Mock DNAFingerPrintService mockService;
```

```
@Mock DNAFingerPrintServiceServiceLocator mockLocator;

@Before
public void setup() throws ServiceException {
  invoker = new DNAFingerPrintWsInvoker(){
    protected DNAFingerPrintServiceServiceLocator
      getServiceLocator() {
      return mockLocator;
    }
  };

  when(mockLocator.getDNAFingerPrintService()).
    thenReturn(mockService);
}

@Test
public void finds_DNA_match() throws Exception {
  when(mockService.findMatch(isA(DNAProfile.class))).
    thenReturn("Sherlock");
  assertEquals("Sherlock", invoker.findMatch
    (new DNAProfile()));
}
}
```

We created a fake instance of the invoker to return a mock service locator class, stubbed the service locator to return a mock web service, and finally, from the JUnit test, we stubbed the mock service to return the name Sherlock for any DNA profile.

9. We are done with client-side JUnit testing; now its time to verify the integration. Rerun the web application and create a JUnit test to invoke the service. Create a source folder slowtest and add the test DNAFingerPrintWsInvokerIntegrationTest under the com.packt. webservice.jaxws.client package. The following is the integration test. Do you remember we hardcoded the web service to return sujoy? Check the DNAFingerPrintService class at step 5. You need to make sure that you still have the web service running at this stage, as we should not break the functionality for JUnit testing.

```
public class DNAFingerPrintWsInvokerIntegrationTest {
  DNAFingerPrintWsInvoker invoker;

  @Before
  public void setup() throws ServiceException {
    invoker = new DNAFingerPrintWsInvoker();
```

```
        }

        @Test
        public void finds_DNA_match() throws Exception {
          assertEquals("sujoy", invoker.findMatch(new
            DNAProfile()));
        }
      }
```

The following is the integration test output:

We are done with the testing and client validation. We can start writing JUnit for the server side; but the server-side code is not tied up with the web service APIs, so we can easily write the JUnit test for the server side, hence skipping the topic.

Developing a RESTful web service

> *Representational State Transfer (REST) is an architectural style consisting of a coordinated set of architectural constraints applied to components, connectors, and data elements, within a distributed hypermedia system.*

REpresentational State Transfer (REST) / **RESTful** web services are built to work best on the Web. REST is an architectural style that specifies constraints (such as the uniform interface) that, if applied to a web service, induces desirable properties, such as performance, scalability, and modifiability, which enable services to work best on the Web.

In REST, architectural data and functionality are considered resources and are accessed using **Uniform Resource Identifiers (URIs)** and hyperlinks on the Web. The REST architectural style has a constraint to have a stateless HTTP communication protocol in a client/server architecture. In the REST architectural style, clients and servers exchange representations of resources by using a standardized interface and protocol.

Basically, RESTful web services consist of the following components:

- **Resource URLs**: A resource URL represents a resource. Basically, a noun is used to represent a resource, for example, a collection of resources can be represented as `http://my.colleage.com/students/` and a specific resource can be represented as `http://my.colleage.com/students/101`.

- **Operations/HTTP headers**: RESTful web services use the following HTTP headers:

  ○ POST: This signifies a CREATE operation or a new resource creation. For example, an HTTP **POST** operation on the `http://my.colleage.com/students` URL with the following data will create a student with the roll number 102:

    ```
    {
      "roleNumber": "102",
      "name": "Bob Biswas",
      "class" : "XII",
      "email" : "bob.sawsib@gmail.com"
    }
    ```

  ○ GET: This implies a READ operation. For example, an HTTP **GET** operation on the `http://my.colleage.com/students` URL will return the following data:

    ```
    {
      students =[
        {
          "roleNumber": "101",
          "name": "Leo Anthony",
          "class" : "X",
          "email" : "leo.p@someemail.com"
        },
        {
          "roleNumber": "102",
          "name": "Bob Biswas",
          "class" : "XII",
          "email" : "bob.sawsib@gmail.com"
        },
    }
    ```

  ○ PUT: This stands for the MODIFY/UPDATE operation. For example, an HTTP **PUT** operation that can help us to update the e-mail ID of the student whose roll number is 101.

° DELETE: This represents a DELETE operation. For example, an HTTP **DELETE** operation on the `http://my.colleage.com/students/101` URL will delete the student whose roll number is `101`.

The main PUT/POST difference
PUT is idempotent, so repeated PUT operations result in the same thing, whereas repeated POST operations may perform repeated actions.

- **Media types**: **Hypermedia as the Engine of Application State (HATEOAS)** is a constraint of the REST application architecture. A hypermedia-driven site provides information to navigate the site's REST interfaces dynamically by including hypermedia links with the responses. The responses of a RESTful web service are media types such as JSON or XML.

- **HTTP status codes**: Every RESTful web service call returns a status code. The status codes given in the following table are very useful:

Status code	Description
200	OK
201	Created
202	Accepted
203	Non-authoritative Information
204	No Content
205	Reset Content
300	Multiple Choices
304	Not Modified
400	Bad Request
401	Unauthorized
403	Forbidden
404	Not Found
405	Method Not Allowed
408	Request Timeout
409	Conflict
500	Internal Server Error
501	Not Implemented

For RESTful web service details, visit the following URL:
`http://docs.oracle.com/javaee/6/tutorial/doc/gijqy.html`

Building a RESTful web service with Spring Framework

Spring MVC was built to provide a flexible framework for web application developers. Spring's `DispatcherServlet` class acts as a front controller; it receives all the incoming requests and delegates the processing of the requests to handlers. It allows developers to concentrate on business logic rather than work on the boilerplate of a custom front controller. This section describes the Spring MVC architecture and how RESTful web applications can be unit tested using Spring MVC.

In Spring MVC, the following is a pattern of a simplified request handling mechanism:

1. `DispatcherServlet` receives a request, confers with handler mappings to find out which controller can handle the request, and then passes the request to the selected controller.

2. The selected controller performs the business logic (can delegate the request to a service or business logic processor) and returns some information back to `DispatcherServlet` for user display or response. Instead of sending the information (model) directly to the user, the controller returns a view name that can render the model.

3. `DispatcherServlet` then resolves the physical view from the view name and passes the model object to the view. This way, `DispatcherServlet` is decoupled from the view implementation. The view renders the model. A view could be a JSP page, a servlet, a PDF file, an Excel report, or any presentable component.

   The following sequence diagram represents the flow and interaction of the Spring MVC components:

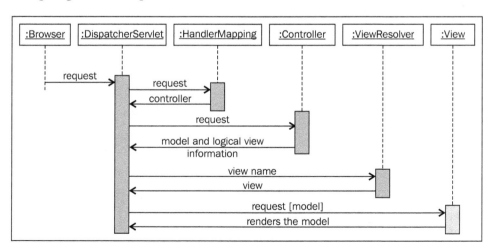

For a RESTful web service, instead of forwarding the model and the view object or the logical view name from controller, we can directly return response data from the controller using Spring's `@ResponseBody` annotation.

We'll build a Spring RESTful web service and unit test the code using JUnit. The following are the steps to be performed:

1.   Launch Eclipse and create a dynamic web project named RESTfulStudentWS.

2.   Open `web.xml` and enter the following lines:

```xml
<display-name>RESTfulStudentWS</display-name>
<servlet>
  <servlet-name>rest</servlet-name>
  <servlet-class>
    org.springframework.web.servlet.DispatcherServlet
  </servlet-class>
  <load-on-startup>1</load-on-startup>
</servlet>
<servlet-mapping>
  <servlet-name>rest</servlet-name>
  <url-pattern>/</url-pattern>
</servlet-mapping>
<context-param>
  <param-name>contextConfigLocation</param-name>
  <param-value>
    /WEB-INF/rest-servlet.xml
  </param-value>
</context-param>
</web-app>
```

The dispatcher is named `rest`, and it maps all requests. Note the `contextConfigLocation` parameter; it indicates that the Spring beans are defined in `/WEB-INF/rest-servlet.xml`.

3.   Create an XML file named `rest-servlet.xml` in `WEB-INF` and add the following lines:

```xml
<?xml version="1.0"encoding="UTF-8"?>
<beans xmlns="http://www.springframework.org/schema/beans"
  xmlns:context="http://www.springframework.org/
    schema/context"
  xmlns:xsi="http://www.w3.org/2001/XMLSchema-instance"
  xsi:schemaLocation="http://www.springframework.org
    /schema/beans
    http://www.springframework.org/schema/beans/spring-
      beans-3.0.xsd
```

```
http://www.springframework.org/schema/context
http://www.springframework.org/schema/context/spring-
    context-3.0.xsd">
<context:component-scan base-package="com.packt.
restful.controller" />
<bean class= "org.springframework.web.servlet.view.
    InternalResourceViewResolver">
"" <mvc:annotation-driven />
</beans>
```

The preceding XML code instructs the Spring configuration that all beans are configured under the `com.packt.restful.controller` package with the Spring annotations.

4. Copy the following Spring JAR files from the Spring download site and put them under the `/WEB-INF/lib` folder:

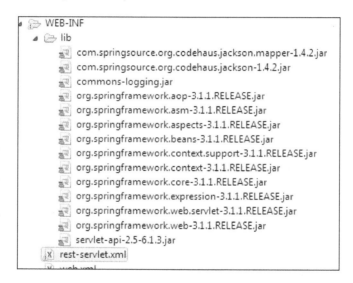

5. Create a Java class `com.packt.restful.model.Student` and add the following members and getters/setters in it:

```
private String roleNumber;
private String name;
private String className;
private String emailId;
```

6. Create a data access class `StudentDao` to mimic the JDBC data access. We'll set up a map of students to bypass the real database interaction. Add the following lines to the `StudentDao` class. Note that the `retrieveAll` and `retrieve(roleId)` methods are public methods for retrieving all the students and a specific student respectively.

```java
@Component
public class StudentDao {

    private Map<String, Student> database = new HashMap
        <String, Student>();
    public StudentDao(){
        load();
    }

    public Collection<Student> retrieveAll() {
        return database.values();
    }

    public Student retrieve(String roleId) {
        return database.get(roleId);
    }

    private void load() {
        Student student = new Student();
        student.setClassName("X");
        student.setEmailId("sujoy@gmaill.com");
        student.setName("Sujoy Acharya");
        student.setRoleNumber("100");
        database.put(student.getRoleNumber(), student);

        student = new Student();
        student.setClassName("XII");
        student.setEmailId("leo.p@gmaiil.com");
        student.setName("Leo Anthony");
        student.setRoleNumber("101");
        database.put(student.getRoleNumber(), student);

        student = new Student();
        student.setClassName("XII");
        student.setEmailId("john.p@ggmail.com");
        student.setName("John Paul");
        student.setRoleNumber("7");
        database.put(student.getRoleNumber(), student);
```

```
      student = new Student();
      student.setClassName("XII");
      student.setEmailId("cs@yahumail.com");
      student.setName("Subodh Chavan");
      student.setRoleNumber("3");
      database.put(student.getRoleNumber(), student);
   }
}
```

7. Create a controller class for exposing the student's data as a RESTful service. Create a `StudentController` class and annotate the class with `@Controller` to notify the Spring framework that the class is a Spring controller class. Also annotate the class with `@RequestMapping("/college")` to map requests for "/college" to `StudentController`. The following is the class:

```
@Controlle
@RequestMapping("/college")
public class StudentController {
   @Autowired StudentDao studentDao;

   @RequestMapping(value = "/students/{roleNumber}", method
      = RequestMethod.GET)
   public @ResponseBody Student retrieve(@PathVariable
      String roleNumber) {
      return studentDao.retrieve(roleNumber);
   }

   @RequestMapping(value = "/students/", method =
      RequestMethod.GET)
   public @ResponseBody List<Student> retrieveAll() {
      return new    ArrayList<Student>(studentDao.
         retrieveAll());
   }
}
```

Note that the methods are annotated with `@RequestMapping`; this annotation maps a URL to a method. An HTTP GET request with the `/college/students/n` URL (where n is a roll number) will be handled by the `retrieve()` method. We can change the method type to POST in order to handle HTTP POST requests; the default method type is GET.

In MVC, controller methods return a model and a view object or a logical view name, but when we annotate a method with `@ResponseBody`, it implies that the response will be sent back directly to the caller instead of getting processed by a view.

8. Start the web application in Tomcat and type the URL `http://localhost:8080/RESTfulStudentWS/college/students/`. Please change the server name and port as per your Tomcat settings. You will get a JSON response back for all the students; the following is the output:

```
localhost:8080/RESTfulStudentWS/college/students/
```
```
[{"name":"Subodh Chavan","className":"XII","emailId":"cs@yahumail.com","roleNumber":"3"},
{"name":"John Paul","className":"XII","emailId":"john.p@ggmail.com","roleNumber":"7"},
{"name":"Leo Anthony","className":"XII","emailId":"leo.p@gmaiil.com","roleNumber":"101"},
{"name":"Sujoy Acharya","className":"X","emailId":"sujoy@gmaill.com","roleNumber":"100"}]
```

9. Now pass a roll number to the URL to get a student's details. The following is the output when we pass 7 as the roll number:

```
localhost:8080/RESTfulStudentWS/college/students/7
```
```
{"name":"John Paul","className":"XII","emailId":"john.p@ggmail.com","roleNumber":"7"}
```

10. When we pass a roll number that doesn't exist, it returns `null`. The following URL passes the number `1000` and gets the following output:

```
localhost:8080/RESTfulStudentWS/college/students/1000
```

In real life application, the `StudentDao` class will be replaced by a real database access class. The real DAO class makes unit testing the controller difficult. Separating the data access layer from the business logic layer helps us change the database without affecting the business logic layer and allows us to unit test the business logic layer in isolation from the database. Suppose you are using the MySQL database and you want to migrate to SQLServer, then you don't have to touch the business logic layer. We'll use Mockito to isolate the DAO layer from the service layer; the following are the steps to be performed:

1. Create a test class `StudentControllerTest` under the source folder `test` and add `mockito-all-1.9.5.jar` to the `lib` folder under `WEB-INF`. The controller class calls the `studentDao` class and Spring autowires the DAO layer to the controller class. We need to modify the controller class to pass as a setter from the JUnit tests. The following is the modified controller class (other methods are skipped for brevity):

```
@Controller
@RequestMapping("/college")
public class StudentController {
  @Autowired
  private StudentDao studentDao;
  public void setStudentDao(StudentDao studentDao) {
    this.studentDao = studentDao;
  }
}
```

2. In the test, create a mock instance of the DAO class and pass it on to the controller as a setter injection. The following is the test:

```
@RunWith(MockitoJUnitRunner.class)
public class StudentControllerTest {
  @Mock
  StudentDao studentDao;

  @InjectMocks
  StudentController controller;
}
```

The `@RunWith(MockitoJUnitRunner.class)` annotation allows us to use the `@Mock` annotation to automatically mock the objects. The `@InjectMocks` annotation injects the mock objects as a setter, constructor, or property injection.

3. Now, stub the `retrieveAll` method of the DAO class to return the students. The following is the modified test:

```
@RunWith(MockitoJUnitRunner.class)
public class StudentControllerTest {
  @Mock
  StudentDao studentDao;

  @InjectMocks
  StudentController controller;

  @Before
  public void  setUp(){
    Student student = new Student();
    student.setClassName("X");
    student.setEmailId("email@mail.com");
    student.setName("sujoy");
    student.setRoleNumber("7");
    Collection<Student> studentColl = new ArrayList
      <Student>();
    studentColl.add(student);
    when(studentDao.retrieveAll()).thenReturn(studentColl);

  }
  @Test
  public void retrieves_students() throws Exception {
    List<Student> retrieveAll = controller.retrieveAll();
    assertFalse(retrieveAll.isEmpty());
  }
}
```

4. Similarly, add more tests to verify that a specific student's details are retrieved when the roll number matches what is passed, and, also, null is returned when the roll number doesn't match. The following is the test:

```
@Test
public void retrieves_a_student() throws Exception {
  when(studentDao.retrieve(eq("100"))).thenReturn(new
    Student());
  assertNotNull(controller.retrieve("100"));
}

@Test
public void when_invalid_role_number_returns_null(){
  assertNull(controller.retrieve("100"));
}
```

Summary

This chapter covered web services, explored SOAP and RESTful web services with examples, and created JUnit tests for the web services with Mockito.

The next chapter, *Unit Testing GWT Code with Mockito*, covers building web applications with **Google Web Toolkit (GWT)**, GWT development patterns, and JUnit testing GWT modules with Mockito.

7

Unit Testing GWT Code with Mockito

"The secret of change is to focus all of your energy, not on fighting the old, but on building the new."

– Socrates

In today's world, Ajax plays an essential role in web application development. **Google Web Toolkit (GWT)** offers internationalization, cross-browser compatibility, Java coding, hosted mode for unit testing the client component in isolation from the server-side component, and so many things, for free. Unit testing the client-side business logic and building a JUnit safety net around the GWT code is very important for code quality and code maintenance. GWT code works with different **Document Object Model (DOM)** widgets and events; business logic gets tied up with the DOM widgets and events and makes it impossible to write unit test for the business logic. Mockito plays a key role in isolating the DOM widgets and events from the logic.

This chapter provides an overview of Ajax/GWT, explains the **Model View Presenter (MVP)** pattern and loose coupling, and provides examples and strategies to mock GWT widgets using Mockito. The following topics are covered in this chapter:

- AJAX/GWT overview
- Developing a small GWT application with the MVP pattern
- Unit testing MVP with Mockito

Exploring Ajax and GWT

AJAX stands for **Asynchronous JavaScript and XML**. Ajax allows content on web pages to update immediately when a user performs any action, unlike an HTTP request, where users must wait for a whole new page to load and be rendered by the web browser. Conventional web applications transmit information to and from the server using synchronous requests. Users fill out a form, hit submit, and get directed to a new page with new information from the server. The user cannot do anything with the web page until the response is back from the server; this means the user is blocked while the request is being processed. In Ajax, JavaScript makes a request to the server, interprets the response, and updates the current screen. The user never gets to know that anything was even transmitted to the server, as the user can continue to use the application while the JavaScript requests information from the server in the background.

Ajax combines numerous tools, such as JavaScript, **Dynamic HTML (DHTML)**, XML, **Cascading Style Sheets (CSS)**, JSON, the DOM, and the Microsoft object, XMLHttpRequest.

The following JavaScript snippet explains an Ajax call and how to handle the result in a JavaScript callback method:

```
function ajaxFunction() {
  var xmlhttp;
  if (window.XMLHttpRequest)  {
    // code for IE7+, Firefox, Chrome, Opera, Safari
    xmlhttp=new XMLHttpRequest();
  } else if (window.ActiveXObject)  {
    // code for IE6, IE5
    xmlhttp=new ActiveXObject("Microsoft.XMLHTTP");
  } else   {
    alert("Your browser does not support XMLHTTP!");
  }
  xmlhttp.onreadystatechange=function() {
    if(xmlhttp.readyState == 4)  {
      // 200 is a successful return
      if(xmlhttp.status == 200){
        alert(xmlhttp.responseText);
      }else{
        alert('Error: '+ xmlhttp.status);
      }
    }
  }
  xmlhttp.open("GET","time.asp",true);
  xmlhttp.send(null);
}
```

The `xmlhttp.responseText` object contains the server response. It could be an document, a simple text, or JSON data. The client-side JavaScript has to process the data as per requirement. To know more about Ajax, visit the following URL:

`https://developer.mozilla.org/en/docs/AJAX`

GWT is a development toolkit for building and optimizing complex browser-based RPC applications. The goal of GWT is to enable productive development of high-performance web applications without the developer having to be an expert in browser quirks, XMLHttpRequest, and JavaScript.

The preceding Ajax example checks the browser version, creates the request object, and makes an asynchronous call. The callback checks the status of the response and processes the response to bind the data to the appropriate DOM object. Ajax response processing needs special care as it handles lots of potential error cases due to network and asynchrony (plus browser incompatibilities), and adds complexity. Maintaining JavaScript code is very difficult as it is dynamic in nature, and because there is no modularization; even the inheritance system using prototype inheritance is both weak and poorly understood. There is no encapsulation, due to which, writing unit tests for JavaScript is not easy. Also, JavaScripts are browser sensitive as each browser doesn't support the same set of JavaScript APIs. GWT provides cross-browser support; we build the application in Java and the GWT compiler translates the Java code into JavaScript that runs on all common browsers. As the code is written in Java, we can write unit tests, refactor code, reuse our existing Java skills, share code with other Java codebases, use Java tools, and gain the things that the Java language is good at, such as static typing and strong OO designs, and build a maintainable software in Java using GWT.

The following are the main advantages of GWT:

- As it is written in Java, it gets Java tool supports such as refactoring, unit testing, seamless integration with continuous integration tools, and Java documentation
- The GWT compiler generates optimized JavaScript code that helps in faster client-side JavaScript execution and performance
- GWT provides cross-browser support; so if your code runs fine in one browser, it will run fine in other common browsers as well
- Maintainable application can be developed using GWT, for example, MVP, MVC, and event bus
- Decent library support and third-party widgets for complex UI development
- Java code can be debugged; the GWT-hosted mode allows us to debug client-side code and also helps us to unit test JavaScript code in isolation from the server code

Visit `http://www.gwtproject.org/` for more information. The next section will explore the MVP pattern.

Learning the MVP pattern

Building an application in an unplanned way suffers many problems, such as adding new features, making a huge effort as the architecture becomes rigid, maintaining the software (activities such as bug fixing) can turn into a nightmare, white box testing or unit testing the code becomes very difficult, and conflict and integration issues when many people work with the same or similar features. Generally, if no thought is given to refactoring as you go, the architecture may become a big ball of mud, and without planning, you may end up with a poor structure that might become difficult to change. To overcome these issues, we can employ many design patterns, such as MVC and MVP. GWT development goes very well with the MVP pattern as it allows loose coupling and separation of concerns.

The MVP approach divides the code into layers that solve the issues with code. MVP believes in separation of concerns and proposes the following logical layers:

- **Model**: A model encompasses business objects or data.

- **View**: A view contains all of the UI components that make up our application. This includes any tables, labels, buttons, textboxes, and so on. Views are responsible for the layout of the UI components and have no notion of the model. That is to say a view doesn't know that it is displaying a house or kangaroo; it simply knows that it has a label, two textboxes, and two buttons that are organized in a vertical or horizontal fashion.

  Switching between views is tied to the history management within the presentation layer.

- **Presenter**: A presenter manages the views while updating the models when necessary. A presenter contains all of the logic for the application, including history management, view transition, and data synchronization via **Remote Procedure Calls (RPCs)** back to the server. In general, every view is driven by a presenter and it handles events that are sourced from the UI widgets within the view. RPC is an inter-process communication, which allows the GWT code to cause a Java process or procedure to execute in another address space.

The following figure represents the MVP components:

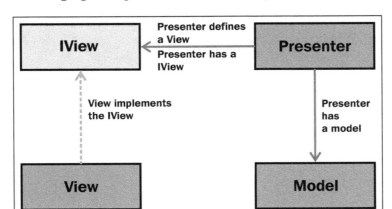

The presenter contains a view interface and a model. A concrete view is created and passed to the presenter; the presenter doesn't know about the concrete view, but it can access the methods of the view through the view interface. The view interface defines methods to render data, update the view, or access a DOM component of the view, but the interface should not return a low-level DOM component to the presenter. If a view contains a button, the interface should define a method to get hold of the button, but the method shouldn't return the button type; instead, it should return a high-level DOM component, such as clickable. The view doesn't handle the DOM events; the presenter implements the DOM event handling; for example, it will create a click event handler and set it to the button's handler list. That way, the view doesn't contain any logic. The presenter manages event handling and view transition. For example, consider a word processor application that has a view for listing all documents and has an edit button for editing a selected document. On the edit button, when you click on current (the list documents presenter), the presenter needs to change the view to the edit mode and open the document for editing. The list document presenter will fire an event so that another presenter can handle the edit operation. An edit document presenter will take care of the view. The presenter can update the model and send it to view for updating the view, such as a presenter making an asynchronous call to the server to get the updated stock price; on service callback, it will update the model with the latest data and call the view to update the new information.

The next section will demonstrate a GWT application and explain the MVP details.

Developing a GWT application using MVP

We'll develop an application in Eclipse. Visit the following URL to download the
Google Plugin for Eclipse:

```
https://developers.google.com/eclipse/docs/download
```

Install the plugin and create a new web application. The following screenshot
shows this:

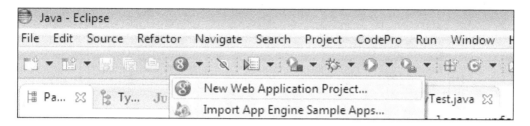

A new application wizard will appear on the screen. To create a new web
application, perform the following steps:

1. Enter the project name as `OutstandingBills` and the package name as `com.packt.billing`.

2. Check the **Google SDKs** checkbox and select the default SDK radio button.

3. If you have downloaded a separate GWT binary, provide the path and
    configure the SDK. Also, check the **Generate project sample code** checkbox;
    it will create the necessary files we need to develop a GWT application. We'll
    change the filenames as required.

    The following screenshot displays the settings:

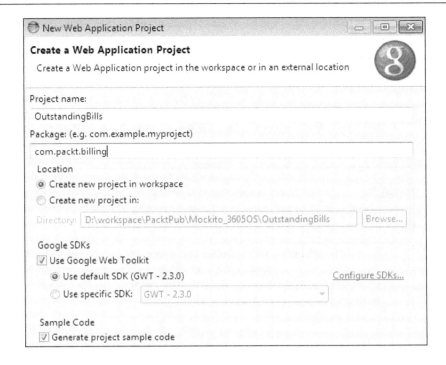

The preceding steps will generate the following project structure:

4. Open the `OutstandingBill.gwt.xml` file; this file contains the project metadata, for example, the `<entry-point>` classname. The `EntryPoint` is the starting point in GWT applications.

5. Open the `com.packt.billing.client.OutstandingBills` entry-point class. It implements the `EntryPoint` interface and overrides the `onModuleLoad()` method. This method is invoked during a GWT application loading.

   GWT applications make asynchronous calls to the server and process responses with service callbacks. When the server response comes back, a callback processes the response. All callbacks implement the `AsyncCallback` interface and the `onSuccess()` and `onFailure()` methods. The `onFailure` method is called when the server encounters any error and throws an exception or error. The `onFailure` method can take care of the server failure, for example, it can show a proper error message to the user. The `onSuccess` method is called when the server returns a response and no error occurs on the server side.

6. Check that Eclipse has generated two interfaces, `GreetingService` and `GreetingServiceAsync`, for service invocation. Conventionally, the `<ServiceName>Service` interface defines the service methods and extends the `RemoteService` interface as follows:

```
@RemoteServiceRelativePath("greet")
public interface GreetingService extends RemoteService {
   String greetServer(String name) throws IllegalArgument
     Exception;
}
```

   A server-side class implements the interface.

   The other `<ServiceName>ServiceAsync` interface redefines the method, but all methods become void; yet they all take an additional parameter called `AsyncCallback`:

```
public interface GreetingServiceAsync {
   void greetServer(String input, AsyncCallback<String>
     callback)
   throws IllegalArgumentException;
}
```

   Note that `greetServer()` is a void method and it takes an additional parameter's `AsyncCallback<String>` callback. If a service method returns `ArrayList<Integer>`, the callback will look like `AsyncCallback<ArrayList<Integer>>`. We would rather define the service interface and the async interface relation as follows:

```
@RemoteServiceRelativePath("name")
public interface SomeService extends RemoteService {
   T someMethod(String name) throws E;
}
```

In the preceding code, `T` is any Java type, such as object, integer, or string, and `E` is any exception, such as `IllegalStateException`.

The async interface will look like the following code snippet:

```
public interface SomeServiceAsync {
  void someMethod (String input, AsyncCallback<T> callback)
    throws E;
}
```

7. The GWT compiler translates the Java code to JavaScript. Select the project and click on the red-colored **GWT Compile** icon from the toolbar, or you can right-click on the project and then select **Google** from the pop-up menu and click on the **GWT Compile** menu item, as shown in the following screenshot:

The preceding step will compile the code and generate JavaScript under the `war` folder; the following screenshot displays the location:

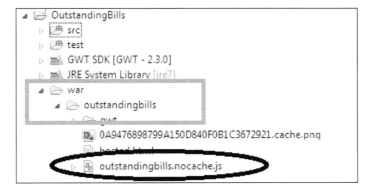

Note that the compilation has generated a JavaScript file called `outstandingbills.nocache.js`. This JavaScript file is responsible for rendering the application. From the HTML or JSP file, you need to provide the path of the script file, as shown in the following line of code:

```
<script type="text/javascript" language="javascript" src
  ="outstandingbills/outstandingbills.nocache.js"></script>
```

We'll now build an application to handle outstanding hotel bills. The user interface will display a textbox and a **Query Bill** button. The user will enter a room number and then hit the button to query the current outstanding bill. A pop up will be displayed with the bill details and payment options. The following are the steps to build the application:

1. Create a serializable class `Bill` in the `com.packt.billing.client` package, and add the following members and getters/setters:

   ```
   private String details;
   private BigDecimal payable;
   ```

2. Create a service interface to retrieve the outstanding bills and make the payment. Create a `BillingService` interface in the `com.packt.billing.client` package with the following details:

   ```
   @RemoteServiceRelativePath("bill")
   public interface BillingService extends RemoteService {
     public Bill retrieve(String roomNumber);
     public boolean pay(String roomNumber, BigDecimal amount);
   }
   ```

3. Create an async interface with the following information:

   ```
   public interface BillingServiceAsync {
     public void retrieve(String roomNumber, AsyncCallback
       <Bill> callback);
     public void pay(String roomNumber, BigDecimal amount,
       AsyncCallback<Boolean> callback);
   }
   ```

4. Create a service implementation class `com.packt.billing.server.BillingServiceImpl`, implementing `BillingService`:

   ```
   @SuppressWarnings("serial")
   public class BillingServiceImpl extends RemoteServiceServlet
   implements BillingService {
     @Override
     public Bill retrieve(String rommNumber) {
       // TODO Auto-generated method stub
       return null;
     }
     @Override
     public boolean pay(String roomNumber, BigDecimal amount)
       {
       // TODO Auto-generated method stub
       return false;
     }
   }
   ```

Usually, two separate projects should be created for the GWT service and service implementation, namely, a contract project with service and async interfaces, and an implementation project that implements the service interface. Both the projects should be deployed in the web/application server.

5. Modify the web.xml file under the war folder and add the following entries to define the BillingServiceImpl servlet and to map the URL to BillingServiceImpl. All HTTP requests with the /outstandingbills/bill URL pattern will be mapped to the BillingServiceImpl servlet:

```
<servlet>
  <servlet-name>billingServlet</servlet-name>
  <servlet-class>
    com.packt.billing.server.BillingServiceImpl
  </servlet-class>
</servlet>

<servlet-mapping>
  <servlet-name>billingServlet</servlet-name>
  <url-pattern>/outstandingbills/bill</url-pattern>
</servlet-mapping>
```

6. Open the OutstandingBills class and replace all GreetingService references with BillingService; remove everything from the onModuleLoad() method. The following is the modified class:

```
public class OutstandingBills implements EntryPoint {

  private final BillingServiceAsync service = GWT
    .create(BillingService.class);

  /*** This is the entry point method. ***/
  @Override
  public void onModuleLoad() {
  }
}
```

Did you notice the service definition? The BillingServiceAsync interface is created with GWT.create(BillingService.class). Basically, a remote service proxy is created to talk to the server-side BillingServiceImpl class. The BillingService interface is annotated with @RemoteServiceRelativeP ath("bill"). Any service call will have the /bill token in the URL. We will set up web.xml to map /bill to the BillingServiceImpl servlet.

7. Now modify the `BillingServiceImpl` class to have some hardcoded room numbers and bills. In constructor, populate a HashMap with room numbers and payable bill amounts. We'll use room numbers from 1 to 5000 and generate random payable amounts. The `retrieve` method will look up the HashMap for the outstanding payable and the `pay` method will deduct the amount from the HashMap. The following is the modified class:

```java
public class BillingServiceImpl extends Remote
  ServiceServlet     implements BillingService {
  private Map<String, BigDecimal> billMap = new
    HashMap<String, BigDecimal>();

  public BillingServiceImpl() {
    Random random = new Random();
    for (int i = 1; i < 5000; i++) {
      billMap.put(String.valueOf(i),new BigDecimal
        (random.nextInt(1000000)));
    }
  }
  @Override
  public Bill retrieve(String roomNumber) {
    BigDecimal payable = billMap.get(roomNumber);
    Bill bill = new Bill();
    if (payable != null) {
      bill.setDetails("Accomodation charge for room#" +
        roomNumber + " and payable amount="+ payable
        .doubleValue());
    }
    bill.setPayable(payable);
    return bill;
  }
  @Override
  public boolean pay(String roomNumber, BigDecimal
    amount) {
    BigDecimal payable = billMap.get(roomNumber);
    if(payable != null){
      payable = payable.subtract(amount);
      billMap.put(roomNumber, payable);
      return true;
    }
    return false;
  }
}
```

We will have two views—the initial query view with the room number textbox and query button, and the bill details view with bill details, payment textbox, and the make payment button; we'll call them QueryView and DetailsView, respectively.

We've already talked about the view interfaces in the MVP section. We'll create two view interfaces with abstract DOM elements, such as HasClickHandlers or HasValue, to represent QueryView and DetailsView in the com.packt.billing.client.view package.

8. We need the room number when the **Query** button is pressed. So we'll add a method to the view to get the room number value. We need to intercept the button click, so we'll add a method to the view to get a clickable object, so that we can add a handler to the object to intercept the button click. The view should not add any handlers to any DOM object. Rather, it should provide the handle to the presenter to handle the logic. The following is the QueryView body:

```
public interface QueryView {
    Widget asWidget();
    HasClickHandlers getQueryButton();
    HasValue<String> getRoomNumber();
}
```

The asWidget() method returns a widget. We'll add the widget to the container. The getQueryButton() method represents the **Query** button and the getRoomNumber() represents the value entered in the room number textbox. Now we need the actual view implementation.

9. Create a QueryViewImpl class in the com.packt.billing.client.view package, implementing the QueryView interface and extending the Composite class:

A Composite class is a type of a widget that can wrap another widget, hiding the wrapped widget's methods. When added to a panel, a Composite class behaves exactly as it should if the widget it wraps had been added. The Composite class is useful for creating a single widget out of an aggregate of multiple other widgets contained in a single panel.

We'll use the `Label`, `TextBox`, `Button`, `FlexTable`, and `HorizontalPanel` GWT widgets to represent the view. The `Label`, `TextBox`, and `Button` GWT widgets will be added to `FlexTable`. Flexible table creates cells on demand. It can be jagged (that is, each row can contain a different number of cells), and individual cells can be set to span multiple rows or columns. The `FlexTable` widget will be added to the `HorizontalPanel` widget. The following is the implementation. The beauty of having a view interface is that you can change the view implementation without altering the code in the presenter. You can use a `Textbox` or `PasswordTextBox` widget to represent `HasValue`; the presenter won't know about the actual implementation. This is how the view is abstracted from the presenter or rather, the view is loosely coupled from the business logic/presenter:

```java
public class QueryViewImpl extends Composite implements
  QueryView {
  private HorizontalPanel mainPanel;
  private TextBox roomNumber= new TextBox();
  private Button query = new Button("Query");

  public QueryViewImpl(){
    mainPanel = new HorizontalPanel();
    mainPanel.setWidth("100%");
    mainPanel.setHorizontalAlignment(HasHorizontalAlignment
      .ALIGN_LEFT);
    FlexTable mainTable = new FlexTable();
    mainTable.setWidth("100%");
    mainTable.setWidget(0, 0, new Label("Room#"));
    mainTable.setWidget(0, 1, roomNumber );
    mainTable.setWidget(0, 2, query );
    mainTable.getCellFormatter().setWidth(0, 0, "5%");
    mainTable.getCellFormatter().setWidth(0, 1, "10%");
    mainPanel.add(mainTable);
    initWidget(mainPanel);
  }

  @Override public Widget asWidget() {
    return this;
  }
}
```

```
@Override public HasClickHandlers getQueryButton() {
    return query;
}

@Override public HasValue<String> getRoomNumber() {
    return roomNumber;
}
}
```

We'll define the view interface and implementation of DetailsView in the next section when the application is up and running with QueryView.

10. Similarly, we need two presenters to present the views. We'll define a Presenter interface in the presenter package with following details:

```
public interface Presenter {
    void render(final HasWidgets container);
}
```

HasWidgets represents a DOM element on the HTML page, such as a <div> element. GWT renders UI components in that DOM container; we'll refer to it as container. The QueryPresenter will present the initial view and implement the Presenter interface. We need to pass a view interface to the presenter, so we'll pass a QueryView instance to the QueryPresenter. The following is the presenter:

```
public class QueryPresenter implements Presenter {
    private final QueryView queryView;

    bv public QueryPresenter(QueryView queryView) {
        this.queryView = queryView;
    }
    @Override public void render(HasWidgets container) {
        container.clear();
        container.add(queryView.asWidget());
    }
}
```

In the next section, we'll create the DetailsPresenter to represent the DetailsView.

11. In a browser, we hit the back button to go back to the previous page. In GWT, there is no previous page, as a single HTML/JSP page displays many views. So to go back or forward to the previous or next view so that we can browse the history. The `com.google.gwt.user.client.History` class represents the browser history. This class allows you to interact with the browser's history stack. Each *item* on the stack is represented by a single string referred to as a *token*. You can create new history items (which have a token associated with them when they are created), and you can programmatically force the current history to move backward or forward.

    History token change is handled by implementing the `ValueChangeHandler<T>` interface:

    ```
    public interface ValueChangeHandler<T> extends
      EventHandler {
      void onValueChange(ValueChangeEvent<T> event);
    }
    ```

    When a history token is changed, the `ValueChangeHandler` interface is notified. However, before that, the handler needs to be registered to `History` using the following syntax:

    ```
    History.addValueChangeHandler(this);
    ```

12. We'll create an `ApplicationController` class. This class will implement the `Presenter` interface and provide the concrete implementation of the `render()` method. Also, the class will implement the `ValueChangeHandler` interface and register itself to `History` to interact with the history. The `render` method will put a new token `START` to the `History` stack to start the view transition. The `onValueChange(ValueChangeEvent event)` method will be invoked on `History` value change; this method will check the token value `START` and create a new `Presenter` interface to display the initial view. The following is the `ApplicationController` class:

    ```
    public class ApplicationController implements Presenter,
      ValueChangeHandler<String>{

      private static final String BLANK = "";
      private static final String START = "START";
      private HasWidgets container;

      public ApplicationController(){
        History.addValueChangeHandler(this);
      }
    }
    ```

The render() method stores the container and checks the History token. If the application is invoked the first time, the History stack will contain a blank string, and then the render() method will add a new token item "START" to the History stack. Otherwise, when you hit refresh, the current state of the History stack is fired so that the same view is rerendered. That way, a user doesn't lose any data. When a new item is pushed or a current history item is fired, the history value changes and then the onValueChange method is invoked:

```
@Override
public void render(HasWidgets container) {
  this.container = container;

  if (BLANK.equals(History.getToken())) {
    History.newItem(START);
  } else {
    History.fireCurrentHistoryState();
  }

}
```

The onValueChange method checks the history token. If the token is "START", it creates the QueryViewImpl view, instantiates the QueryPresenter, and finally, calls the presenter.render() method to display the view. For multiple views, the history token value will be changed, and depending upon the token value, the appropriate presenter will be instantiated and finally, the render() method will be invoked on the presenter:

```
@Override public void onValueChange(ValueChangeEvent
  <String>   event) {
  String token = event.getValue();
  container.clear();
  Presenter presenter = null;
  if (START.equals(token)) {
    presenter = new QueryPresenter(new QueryViewImpl());
  }
  if (presenter != null) {
    presenter.render(container);
  }
}
```

13. Modify the onModuleLoad() method of the OutstandingBills EntryPoint class to create an instance of ApplicationController and invoke the render method with a DOM ID. The following is the modified method:

```
@Override
public void onModuleLoad() {
  Presenter presenter = new ApplicationController();
  presenter.render(RootPanel.get("dom"));
}
```

14. Modify the OutstandingBills.html file to add a div with id="dom":

```html
<html>
  <head>
    <meta http-equiv="content-type" content="text/html;
      charset=UTF-8">

    <link type="text/css" rel="stylesheet" href=
      "OutstandingBills.css">


    <script type="text/javascript" language="javascript"
      src="outstandingbills/outstandingbills.nocache.js"/>

  </head>

  <body>

    <iframe src="javascript:''" id="__gwt_historyFrame"
      tabIndex='-1'style="position:absolute;width:0;
      height:0;border:0">
    </iframe>

    <h1>Web Application Starter Project</h1>

    <div id="dom"></div>
  </body>
</html>
```

Note that the <script> tag loads the GWT script and the <iframe> tag enables the history mechanism. If this entry is missing, the history token management will not work and the MVP pattern's purpose will be violated.

15. Right-click on the project and run it as GWT web application, then copy the URL and paste it to a web browser. The following output will be displayed:

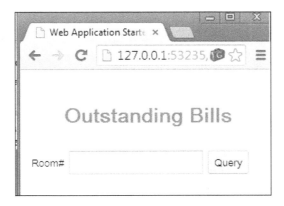

16. Now we have the application configured. The next step is to build the `DetailsView` interface and enable the view transition. We'll start with the new view. Create an interface `DetailsView` and add the following lines:

```
public interface DetailsView {
    Widget asWidget();
    HasClickHandlers getPaymentButton();
    HasClickHandlers getCloseButton();
    HasValue<String> getPaymentAmount();
    void populate(Bill bill);
}
```

The `populate()` method is used to populate the bill details to the UI, the `getCloseButton()` method is used to get hold of the close button, the `getPaymentButton()` method is for the payment button, the `getPaymentAmount()` method is for the payment textbox, and the `asWidget` method is used to return the composite.

17. Create the `DetailsViewImpl` class for displaying the `details` view. The following is the code:

```
public class DetailsViewImpl extends Composite implements
    DetailsView {
    private VerticalPanel mainPanel;
    private TextBox amount = new TextBox();
    private Button payment = new Button("Pay");
    private Button close = new Button("Close");
    private Label desc = new Label();
    private Label dueAmt = new Label();
```

```java
public DetailsViewImpl() {
  mainPanel = new VerticalPanel();
  mainPanel.setWidth("100%");

  FlexTable mainTable = new FlexTable();
  mainTable.setWidth("100%");

  mainTable.setWidget(0,0, new Label("Desc#"));
  mainTable.setWidget(0,1, desc);

  mainTable.setWidget(1,0, new Label("Due#"));
  mainTable.setWidget(1,1, dueAmt);

  mainTable.setWidget(2,0,new Label("Pay amount#"));
   mainTable.setWidget(2,1, amount);

  mainTable.setWidget(3,0, payment);
  mainTable.setWidget(3,1, close);

  mainTable.getCellFormatter().setWidth(0,0, "5%");
  mainTable.getCellFormatter().setWidth(0,1, "60%");

  mainTable.getCellFormatter().setWidth(1,0, "5%");
  mainTable.getCellFormatter().setWidth(1,1, "60%");

  mainTable.getCellFormatter().setWidth(2,0, "5%");
  mainTable.getCellFormatter().setWidth(2,1, "60%");

  mainTable.getCellFormatter().setWidth(3,0, "25%");
  mainTable.getCellFormatter().setWidth(3,1, "60%");

  mainTable.getCellFormatter().setAlignment(3, 0,
    HasHorizontalAlignment.ALIGN_RIGHT,
    HasVerticalAlignment.ALIGN_MIDDLE);

  mainTable.getCellFormatter().setAlignment(3, 1,
    HasHorizontalAlignment.ALIGN_LEFT,
    HasVerticalAlignment.ALIGN_MIDDLE);

  mainPanel.add(mainTable);
  initWidget(mainPanel);
}

@Override public Widget asWidget() {
  return this;
```

```
  }

  @Override public HasClickHandlers getPaymentButton() {
    return payment;
  }

  @Override public HasValue<String> getPaymentAmount() {
    return amount;
  }

  @Override public void populate(Bill bill) {
    desc.setText(bill.getDetails());
    dueAmt.setText(""+bill.getPayable().doubleValue());
  }

  @Override public HasClickHandlers getCloseButton() {
    return close;
  }
}
```

GWT fires GwtEvents to indicate the completion of the task. The class, com. google.gwt.event.shared.GwtEvent, represents the event. This is the root of all GWT events. The user can create custom events to notify if a view change is required (to interact with other views).

An event is always defined with an event handler such as the following:

```
public class SearchEvent extends GwtEvent
  <SearchEventHandler> {
}
```

Every event comes up with an event handling contract. This contract is known as an **event handler**.

Event handlers extend a marker interface com.google.gwt.event.shared. EventHandler.

The following is an example of an event handler contract:

```
public interface SearchEventHandler extends EventHandler {
  void onSearch(SearchEvent event);
}
```

Events are fired to an event bus class: com.google.gwt.event.shared. HandlerManager.

HandlerManager (also known as event bus) is responsible for adding handlers to event sources and associating those handlers to pass in events.

The following code snippet is an example of firing events:

```
eventBus.fireEvent(new SearchEvent(getSearchText()));
```

The following is an example of event handling:

```
eventBus.addHandler(SearchEvent.TYPE, new
  SearchEventHandler() {
  public void onSearch(SearchEvent event) {
    doSearch(event.getRoomNumber());
  }
});
```

In an MVP context, when a presenter needs to notify a view change to the system, it fires a GWT event.

The event handler associated with this event intercepts the event and hands over the control to another presenter. This new presenter renders a new view.

Our `QueryView` needs to notify the view change when the user hits the **Query** button. We'll create a GWT event called `SearchEvent` and a `SearchEventHandler`:

```
public class SearchEvent extends GwtEvent
  <SearchEventHandler> {
  private String roomNumber;

  public static Type<SearchEventHandler> TYPE = new
    Type<SearchEventHandler>();

  @Override
  public com.google.gwt.event.shared.GwtEvent.Type
    <SearchEventHandler> getAssociatedType() {
    return TYPE;
  }

  @Override
  protected void dispatch(SearchEventHandler handler) {
    handler.onSearch(this);
  }

  public String getRoomNumber() {
    return roomNumber;
  }

  public void setRoomNumber(String roomNumber) {
```

```
      this.roomNumber = roomNumber;
   }

}
```

The event handler will look like this:

```
public interface SearchEventHandler extends EventHandler {
   void onSearch(SearchEvent event);
}
```

18. We'll modify the QueryPresenter to fire the SearchEvent with the roomNumber when the user hits the **Query** button. To fire the event, the presenter needs an event bus. Modify the constructor to pass a HandlerManager instance. The following is the modified constructor:

```
public QueryPresenter(QueryView view,HandlerManager bus) {
   this.queryView = view;
   this.eventBus = bus;
   queryView.getQueryButton().addClickHandler(new
      ClickHandler() {
      @Override
      public void onClick(ClickEvent event) {
         SearchEvent searchEvent = new SearchEvent();
         searchEvent.setRoomNumber(queryView.getRoomNumber()
            .getValue());
         eventBus.fireEvent(searchEvent);
      }
   });
}
```

19. Modify the ApplicationController to create a HandlerManager instance and pass it to the modified presenter. The following are the modified constructor and class level members for roomNumber and HandlerManager:

```
private HandlerManager eventBus;
private String roomNumber;
public ApplicationController(){
   History.addValueChangeHandler(this);
   this.eventBus = new HandlerManager(this);

   eventBus.addHandler(SearchEvent.TYPE, new Search
      EventHandler() {
      @Override
      public void onSearch(SearchEvent event) {
         roomNumber = event.getRoomNumber();
         History.newItem(SEARCH);
      }
   });
}
```

20. Create a `DetailsPresenter` to handle the view. The presenter needs to make a service call to check the bill, so we need to pass the `BillingServiceAsync` instance to the presenter, and we also need to pass the `roomNumber` string for which the view will be rendered. The following is the presenter:

```java
public class DetailsPresenter implements Presenter {
  private final DetailsView detailsView;
  private final BillingServiceAsync billingService;
  private final String roomNumber;

  public DetailsPresenter(BillingServiceAsync
    billingService, DetailsView detailsView, String
    roomNumber) {
    this.detailsView = detailsView;
    this.billingService = billingService;
    this.roomNumber = roomNumber;
  }

  @Override
  public void render(final HasWidgets container) {
    container.clear();
    container.add(detailsView.asWidget());


    billingService.retrieve(roomNumber, new
      AsyncCallback<Bill>(){

      @Override
      public void onSuccess(Bill bill) {
        detailsView.populate(bill);
      }

      @Override
      public void onFailure(Throwable caught) {
        Window.alert("Error occured "+caught);
      }
    });
  }
}
```

The `render()` method makes a service call to get the bill information and then passes that information to the view by making a call to the `populate()` method.

21. Modify the `ApplicationController` to intercept the history value change for the `Search` token. Modify the constructor to inject the `BillingService` interface:

```
public ApplicationController(BillingServiceAsync
  billingService){
  this.billingServiceAsync = billingService;
}
```

Modify the `onValueChange()` method to handle the `Search` history token class.

```
@Override
public void onValueChange(ValueChangeEvent<String> event) {
  String token = event.getValue();
  container.clear();
  Presenter presenter = null;
  if (START.equals(token)) {
    presenter = new QueryPresenter(new QueryViewImpl(),
      eventBus);
  }

  if(SEARCH.equals(token)){
    presenter = new DetailsPresenter(billingServiceAsync,
      new DetailsViewImpl(), roomNumber);
  }
  if (presenter != null) {
    presenter.render(container);
  }
}
```

The following will be the output of the new changes:

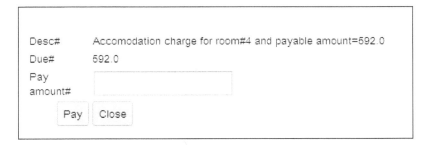

22. Modify the `DetailsPresenter` interface to handle the **Pay** and **Close** button click. On the **Pay** button click, we'll make a service call, display the message, and close the view. On the **Close** button click, we'll put a START item to the history to go back to the initial state. The following is the modified constructor:

```
public DetailsPresenter(BillingServiceAsync service,
  DetailsView view, String rn) {
  this.detailsView = view;
  this.billingService = service;
  this.roomNumber = rn;

  detailsView.getCloseButton().addClickHandler(new
    ClickHandler() {

    @Override public void onClick(ClickEvent event) {
      History.newItem("START");
    }
  });

  detailsView.getPaymentButton().addClickHandler(new
    ClickHandler() {

    @Override
    public void onClick(ClickEvent event) {
      String amount = detailsView.getPaymentAmount()
        .getValue();
      billingService.pay(roomNumber, new BigDecimal
        (amount), new AsyncCallback<Boolean>() {

        @Override
        public void onFailure(Throwable caught) {
          Window.alert("Error "+caught);
        }

        @Override
        public void onSuccess(Boolean result) {
          if(result){
            Window.alert("Posted payment");
            History.newItem("START");
          }else{
            Window.alert("Could not post payment");
          }
        }
      });
    }
  });
}
```

We are done with MVP. We should add the validation logic for user entry fields for blank or invalid input. For instance, an error message should be displayed when the room number textbox is blank but a user hits the **Query** button, or when the payment amount textbox is blank and a user hits the **Pay** button.

Unit testing the GWT code

MVP's loose coupling enables rapid development, as the view implementation, server-side service implementation, and presenters are independent of each other. Hence, developers can concentrate on different areas of the application without stepping on each other, for instance, one can work on the server-side business logic, work on the presentation layer logic, and implement the view logic. View implementation doesn't contain any business logic other than UI components and layout information. So no JUnit test is required for the view implementation; only manual inspection is good enough. However, the presentation layer contains business logic, such as, a user cannot post a negative amount while making the payment for a bill or the payment amount cannot exceed the payable amount. Mockito plays a key role in mocking DOM widgets and stubbing widget behaviors. We'll refactor the `DetailsPresenter` class and extract the anonymous DOM click handler out of the constructor and create a new handler class. The following `ClickHandler` class performs the validation logic:

```
public class PaymentButtonClickHandler implements ClickHandler {
  private DetailsPresenter presenter;
  public PaymentButtonClickHandler(DetailsPresenter
    detailsPresenter) {
    this.presenter = detailsPresenter;
  }

  @Override
  public void onClick(final ClickEvent event) {
    String amount = presenter.getDetailsView().
      getPaymentAmount().getValue();
    if(amount == null || "".equals(amount)){
      Window.alert("Please enter a payment amount");
      return;
    }

    BigDecimal paymentAmt = null;
    try{
      double amtDbl = Double.parseDouble(amount);
      paymentAmt = new BigDecimal(amtDbl);
    }catch(NumberFormatException exception){
```

```
            Window.alert("Please enter a valid payment amount");
            return;
        }
        if(paymentAmt.compareTo(BigDecimal.ZERO) <= 0){
            Window.alert("Please enter a positive payment amount");
            return;
        }

        if(presenter.getDetailsView().getOutstandingAmount()
            .compareTo(paymentAmt) < 0){
            Window.alert("Payment amount cannot exceed the payable
                amount");
            return;
        }
        ((Button)event.getSource()).setEnabled(false);
        presenter.makePayment(paymentAmt);
    }
}
```

Modify the `DetailsPresenter` class to call this click handler. Create a JUnit test `PaymentButtonClickHandlerTest` under the `test` source folder and the `com.packt.billing.client.event` package. You cannot mock the static call to the `Window.alert()` method. If you just write `Window.alert()` in your JUnit test and run the test, you will encounter an `UnsatisfiedLinkError` exception, as shown in the following screenshot:

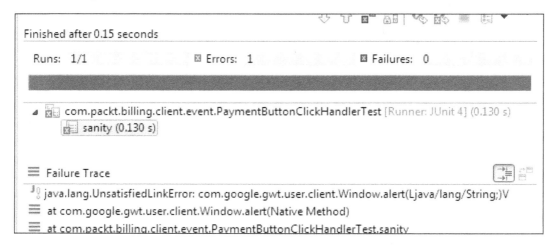

We'll use PowerMock to disable the static calls to the `Window.alert()` method. Add the associated JAR files to the project classpath and modify the test as follows:

```
@RunWith(PowerMockRunner.class)
@PrepareForTest(Window.class)
public class PaymentButtonClickHandlerTest {

  PaymentButtonClickHandler handler;
  @Mock
  DetailsPresenter mockPresenter;
  ArgumentCaptor<String> captor = null;
  @Before
  public void before() throws Exception{
    GWTMockUtilities.disarm();
    captor = ArgumentCaptor.forClass(String.class);
    handler = new PaymentButtonClickHandler(mockPresenter);
    mockStatic(Window.class);
    PowerMockito.doNothing().when(Window.class, "alert",
      captor.capture());
  }

  @After
  public void after(){
    GWTMockUtilities.restore();
  }

  @Test
  public void sanity() throws Exception {
    Window.alert("dd");
  }
}
```

Google provides the `com.google.gwt.junit.GWTMockUtilities` class to facilitate testing without launching any web server. This class provides methods for disabling and enabling `GWT.create()` behavior in isolation from the web server. The `GWTMockUtilities.disarm()` behavior replaces the normal `GWT.create()` behavior with a method that returns `null` instead of throwing a runtime exception. This is to allow JUnit tests to mock classes that make `GWT.create()` calls in their static initializers. `GWTMockUtilities` is not used with `GWTTestCase` and is not used to test widgets themselves. Rather, it is to allow pure Java unit tests of classes that need to manipulate widgets.

In our test, we need to create a mock button to represent the `Payment` button and disable and re-enable the button within our handler code. So, we need to disarm the static initialization.

The `mockStatic(Window.class)` class disables the `Window.alert` calls. The `PowerMockito.doNothing().when(Window.class, "alert", captor.capture())` method is used to capture the arguments passed to the alert method. The following is the modified test with all the error conditions and happy path:

```
@RunWith(PowerMockRunner.class)
@PrepareForTest(Window.class)
public class PaymentButtonClickHandlerTest {

    PaymentButtonClickHandler handler;
    @Mock
    DetailsPresenter mockPresenter;
    ArgumentCaptor<String> captor = null;
    @Mock
    ClickEvent clickEvent;
    @Mock
    DetailsView detailsView;
    @Mock
    HasValue<String> payAmount;
    @Before
    public void before() throws Exception{
        GWTMockUtilities.disarm();
        when(mockPresenter.getDetailsView()).thenReturn(detailsView);
        when(detailsView.getPaymentAmount()).thenReturn(payAmount);
        handler = new PaymentButtonClickHandler(mockPresenter);
        mockStatic(Window.class);
        captor = ArgumentCaptor.forClass(String.class);
        doNothing().when(Window.class, "alert", captor.capture());
    }

    @After
    public void after(){
        GWTMockUtilities.restore();
    }

    @Test
    public void when_empty_payment_amount_then_raises_error() {
        handler.onClick(clickEvent);
        assertEquals(PLEASE_ENTER_A_PAYMENT_AMOUNT,captor.getValue());
    }

    @Test
    public void when_invalid_payment_amount_then_raises_error() {
        when(payAmount.getValue()).thenReturn("abc$$$");
```

```
    handler.onClick(clickEvent);
    assertEquals(PLEASE_ENTER_A_VALID_PAYMENT_AMOUNT,
      captor.getValue());
  }

  @Test
  public void when_zero_payment_amount_then_raises_error(){
    when(payAmount.getValue()).thenReturn("0.00");
    handler.onClick(clickEvent);
    assertEquals(PLEASE_ENTER_A_POSITIVE_PAYMENT_AMOUNT,
      captor.getValue());
  }

  @Test
  public void when_negative_payment_amount_then_raises_error(){
    when(payAmount.getValue()).thenReturn("-10.00");
    handler.onClick(clickEvent);
    assertEquals(PLEASE_ENTER_A_POSITIVE_PAYMENT_AMOUNT,
      captor.getValue());
  }

  @Test
  public void when_payment_amount_exceeds_the_payable_then_raises
    _error(){
    when(payAmount.getValue()).thenReturn("100.00");
    when(detailsView.getOutstandingAmount()).thenReturn(new
      BigDecimal("50.00"));
    handler.onClick(clickEvent);
    assertEquals(PAYMENT_AMOUNT_CANNOT_EXCEED_THE_PAYABLE_AMOUNT
      ,captor.getValue());
  }

  @Test
  public void when_payment_amount_not_greater_than_payable_amount
    _then_posts_the_payment() throws Exception {
    Button pay = PowerMockito.mock(Button.class);

    PowerMockito.when(clickEvent.getSource()).thenReturn(pay);
    when(payAmount.getValue()).thenReturn("100.00");
    when(detailsView.getOutstandingAmount()).thenReturn(new
      BigDecimal("200.00"));
    handler.onClick(clickEvent);
    verifyStatic(Mockito.never());
  }
}
```

So far, we covered the noninvasive, POJO-based Java unit tests for GWT, but Google provides a `GWTTestCase` class for invasive unit testing that acts as a bridge between the JUnit environment and the GWT environment. The `GWTTestCase` class extends the `TestCase` class. Running a compiled `GWTTestCase` subclass under JUnit launches the `HtmlUnit` browser, which serves to emulate your application behavior during test execution.

The typical way to set up a JUnit test case class is to have it extend `TestCase` and then run it with the JUnit `TestRunner` class. It is a convention to begin the name of all test methods with the prefix `test`. Now we use JUnit 4, which supports noninvasive, POJO-based unit testing and allows us to use annotations instead of conventions, such as a test should be started with the prefix `test`. So `GWTTestCase` is not recommended.

The `HtmlUnit` browser is an open source, GUI-less browser written in 100 percent Java. As `HtmlUnit` does not involve any native code, debugging GWT tests in development mode can be done entirely in a Java debugger. The `HtmlUnit` browser does not require firing up a new browser process; the `HtmlUnit` browser instances just run as new threads. To learn more about `HtmlUnit` or `GWTTestCase`, visit http://www.gwtproject.org/.

Summary

This book has taught you the essentials of Mockito, such as Mockito basics, advanced usage of Mockito APIs, writing BDD with Mockito, handling legacy code with Mockito, mocking web services, and finally, this chapter covered the AJAX and GWT overview, discussed the MVP pattern, built an example of MVP with GWT, isolated DOM widgets from client-side business logic using PowerMockito, and disabled static DOM calls with PowerMockito and GWTMockUtility.

Now you should be able to isolate your business logic from external dependencies using Mockito.

Index

Symbols

@captor annotation
  example 87
@InjectMocks annotation
  example 88, 89
@Mock annotation 44
@spy annotation
  example 88

A

acceptance tests
  URL 100
advanced Mockito 66
advanced Mockito APIs
  annotations 87
  arguments, verifying
      ArgumentCaptor used 81
  default Mockito settings,
      modifying 89-92
  doCallRealMethod method 79
  doNothing method 79
  doReturn() method 79, 80
  exception, throwing from
      void methods 72-74
  inline stubbing 92, 93
  invocation order, verifying 84, 85
  mock details, determining 93, 94
  mock objects, resetting 92
  objects, spying 85, 86
  void method callbacks 75-79
  void methods 66-72
agile methodologies
  about 99
  URL 99

agile team
  scoping feature 99
AJAX
  exploring 162-164
  URL 163
Apache Axis
  JAX-WS, creating with 141-144
Apache Tomcat
  JAX-WS, creating with 141-144
  URL, for installation 140
ArgumentCaptor object
  used, for verifying arguments 81
argument matchers
  using 48, 49
arguments
  verifying, ArgumentCaptor object used 81
arrays
  working with 83
Asynchronous JavaScript and
      XML. *See* **AJAX**

B

bar object 93
BDD
  about 95
  bottom-up strategy, exploring 97
  exercising, with Mockito 100-102
  exploring 99, 100
  gaps, finding 98
  top-down strategy, exploring 96, 97
  URL 102
BDD syntax
  about 102
  willAnswer() method 102
  willCallRealMethod() method 102

will() method 102
willReturn() method 102
willThrow() method 102
Behavior-driven Development. *See* **BDD**
benefits, mocking 38
bottom-up approach
  exploring 97
  used, for developing JAX-WS 140
builder pattern 20

C

Cascading Style Sheets (CSS) 162
CGLib
  URL 60
comparison matchers
  about 50
  equalTo 51
  is 51
  not 51
compound value matchers
  about 51-53
  allOf 52
  anyOf 52
  both 52
  either 52
  not 52
constructor injection 87
contract-first web services.
        See **top-down approach**
contract-last web services.
        See **bottom-up approach**
custom ArgumentMatcher class
  comparison matchers 50
  compound value matchers 51-54
  working with 50

D

database call
  mocking, reasons 77
DDD
  about 99
  URL 99
default Mockito settings
  CALLS_REAL_METHODS 90

  modifying 89-92
  RETURNS_DEEP_STUBS 90-92
  RETURNS_DEFAULTS 89, 90
  RETURNS_MOCKS 89-91
  RETURNS_SMART_NULLS 89, 90
defined constructor
  suppressing, in PowerMock 112
DemoController servlet 66
DispatcherServlet class 152
doCallRealMethod method 79
Document Object Model (DOM) 161
Domain-driven Development. *See* **DDD**
doNothing() method 79
doReturn() method
  exploring 79, 80
dummy objects
  using 11-15
Dynamic HTML (DHTML) 162

E

EasyMock 102
Eclipse
  JAX-WS, exploring with 139-149
  URL, for downloading 11
  URL, for installation 140
enrollToCourse method 19
event handler 181
exceptions
  throwing 47, 48
  throwing, from void methods 72-74

F

fake object
  about 126
  implementing 26-33
faking 126
field injection 87
final classes
  stubbing, in PowerMock 116, 117
  working with, for unit test 130-132
final methods
  stubbing, in PowerMock 115, 116
  working with, for unit test 126, 127

G

Gang of Four (GoF) 128
gaps, BDD
  finding 98
generic collection arguments
  working with 82
Google Plugin for Eclipse
  URL, for downloading 166
Google Web Toolkit (GWT)
  about 161
  advantages 163
  exploring 162-164
GWT application
  developing, MVP pattern used 166-187
GWT code
  about 161
  unit testing, performing
    with Mockito 187-192

H

Hamcrest 50
hamcrest matchers 49
HtmlUnit browser 192
HttpServlet 66
HTTP status codes 151
Hypermedia as the Engine of Application
  State (HATEOAS) 151
HyperText Transfer Protocol (HTTP) 138

I

inline stubbing
  working with 92, 93
invocation order
  verifying 84, 85

J

Java API for RESTful Web Services.
  See JAX-RS
Java API for XML Web Services.
  See JAX-WS
JavaScript Object Notation (JSON) 139
JAX-RS
  about 138

reference link 139
JAX-WS
  about 138
  creating, with Apache Axis 141-144
  creating, with Apache Tomcat 141-144
  developing, using bottom-up approach 140
  developing, using top-down approach 140
  exploring, with Eclipse 139-149
  reference link 139
JBehave
  URL 102
jMock 102

L

legacy 103
legacy code
  about 103, 104
  reference link 104
LoginController class 66, 67

M

matchers
  reference link 49
Maven repository
  URL 40
media types, RESTful web services 151
method calls
  answering 57-59
  no-more interactions, verifying 56
  retrieve method 42-44
  stubbing 40-47
  thenAnswer() method 46
  thenCallRealMethod() method 46
  thenReturn() method 46
  thenReturn(value) method 46
  thenThrow() method 46
  verifying 55
  when() method 46
  zero interactions, verifying 56
method calls, verifying
  about 54
  atLeast(int minNumberOfInvocations) 55
  atLeastOnce() 55
  atMost(int maxNumberOfInvocations) 55
  never() 55

S

Service-oriented Architecture. *See* SOA
servlet-api.<version number>.jar
  URL, for downloading 66
setter injection 87
Simple Object Access Protocol (SOAP) 138
SOA
  about 137, 138
  URL 138
software delivery risks
  best practices, for minimizing 98
software development
  stakeholders 96
Spring Framework
  RESTful web services,
      building with 152-159
Spring MVC 152
stakeholders, software development
  analysts 96
  customers 96
  designers/architects 96
  developers 96
  maintenance team 96
  managers 96
  operational folks 96
  testers 96
static blocks
  exploring, for unit test 134
  suppressing, in PowerMock 109, 110
static methods
  mock circumstances 109
  stubbing, in PowerMock 108, 109
static variables
  exploring, for unit test 134
stubs
  working with 15-18
StudentService class 19
super class constructor
  suppressing, in PowerMock 110-112

T

TDD
  about 99
  URL 99

test automation
  benefits 8
test doubles
  about 10
  dummy objects 11-15
  fake objects 26-33
  mock objects 23-25
  spy 18-22
  stubs 15-18
Test-driven Development. *See* TDD
test failure scenario
  demonstrating 23-25
testing impediments
  exploring 104, 105
testing-unfriendly behaviors
  examples 38
test spy
  exploring 18-22
top-down approach
  exploring 96, 97
  used, for developing JAX-WS 140

U

Uniform Resource Identifiers (URIs) 149
unit tests
  characteristics 9
  constructor issues, identifying 119-121
  designing, with Mockito 118
  final classes, working with 130-132
  final methods, working with 126, 127
  initialization issues, realizing 122, 123
  new operator, usage concerns 132, 133
  performing, on GWT code
      with Mockito 187-192
  principles 36, 37
  private methods, working with 123-125
  static blocks, exploring 134
  static method issues, exploring 128-130
  static variables, exploring 134
  working with 8

V

variable arguments
  working with 83
verify() method 54

Thank you for buying
Mockito Essentials

About Packt Publishing

Packt, pronounced 'packed', published its first book "*Mastering phpMyAdmin for Effective MySQL Management*" in April 2004 and subsequently continued to specialize in publishing highly focused books on specific technologies and solutions.

Our books and publications share the experiences of your fellow IT professionals in adapting and customizing today's systems, applications, and frameworks. Our solution based books give you the knowledge and power to customize the software and technologies you're using to get the job done. Packt books are more specific and less general than the IT books you have seen in the past. Our unique business model allows us to bring you more focused information, giving you more of what you need to know, and less of what you don't.

Packt is a modern, yet unique publishing company, which focuses on producing quality, cutting-edge books for communities of developers, administrators, and newbies alike. For more information, please visit our website: www.packtpub.com.

About Packt Open Source

In 2010, Packt launched two new brands, Packt Open Source and Packt Enterprise, in order to continue its focus on specialization. This book is part of the Packt Open Source brand, home to books published on software built around Open Source licenses, and offering information to anybody from advanced developers to budding web designers. The Open Source brand also runs Packt's Open Source Royalty Scheme, by which Packt gives a royalty to each Open Source project about whose software a book is sold.

Writing for Packt

We welcome all inquiries from people who are interested in authoring. Book proposals should be sent to author@packtpub.com. If your book idea is still at an early stage and you would like to discuss it first before writing a formal book proposal, contact us; one of our commissioning editors will get in touch with you.

We're not just looking for published authors; if you have strong technical skills but no writing experience, our experienced editors can help you develop a writing career, or simply get some additional reward for your expertise.

Test-Driven Development with Mockito

ISBN: 978-1-78328-329-3   Paperback: 172 pages

Learn how to apply Test-Driven Development and the Mockito framework in real life projects, using realistic, hands-on examples

1.   Start writing clean, high-quality code to apply design patterns and principles.

2.   Add new features to your project by applying Test-first development — JUnit 4.0 and Mockito framework.

3.   Make legacy code testable and clean up technical debts.

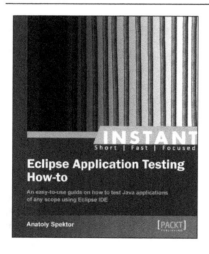

Instant Eclipse Application Testing How-to

ISBN: 978-1-78216-324-4   Paperback: 62 pages

An easy-to-use guide on how to test Java applications of any scope using Eclipse IDE

1.   Learn something new in an Instant! A short, fast, focused guide delivering immediate results.

2.   Learn how to install Eclipse and Java for any platform.

3.   Get to grips with how to efficiently navigate in the Eclipse environment using shortcuts.

Please check **www.PacktPub.com** for information on our titles

Instant Mockito

ISBN: 978-1-78216-797-6   Paperback: 66 pages

Learn how to create stubs, mocks, and spies and verify their behavior using Mockito

1. Learn something new in an Instant! A short, fast, focused guide delivering immediate results.

2. Stub methods with callbacks.

3. Verify the behavior of test mocks.

4. Assert the arguments passed to functions of mocks.

Instant Mock Testing with PowerMock

ISBN: 978-1-78328-995-0   Paperback: 82 pages

Discover unit testing using PowerMock

1. Learn something new in an Instant! A short, fast, focused guide delivering immediate results.

2. Understand how to test unit code using PowerMock, through hands-on examples.

3. Learn how to avoid unwanted behavior of code using PowerMock for testing.

Please check **www.PacktPub.com** for information on our titles

www.ingramcontent.com/pod-product-compliance
Lightning Source LLC
LaVergne TN
LVHW081341050326
832903LV00024B/1249